WHAT ARE YOU HERE TO HEAL?

A Deeper Conversation

Katherine G. Bridge, M.S.W.

BALBOA.
PRESS
A DIVISION OF HAY HOUSE

Balboa Press books may be ordered through booksellers or by contacting:

Balboa Press
A Division of Hay House
1663 Liberty Drive
Bloomington, IN 47403
www.balboapress.com
1 (877) 407-4847

Because of the dynamic nature of the Internet, any web addresses or links contained in this book may have changed since publication and may no longer be valid. The views expressed in this work are solely those of the author and do not necessarily reflect the views of the publisher, and the publisher hereby disclaims any responsibility for them.

The author of this book does not dispense medical advice or prescribe the use of any technique as a form of treatment for physical, emotional, or medical problems without the advice of a physician, either directly or indirectly. The intent of the author is only to offer information of a general nature to help you in your quest for emotional and spiritual well-being. In the event you use any of the information in this book for yourself, which is your constitutional right, the author and the publisher assume no responsibility for your actions.

Any people depicted in stock imagery provided by Getty Images are models, and such images are being used for illustrative purposes only.
Certain stock imagery © Getty Images.

Print information available on the last page.

ISBN: 978-1-5043-9905-0 (sc)
ISBN: 978-1-5043-9906-7 (e)

Balboa Press rev. date: 07/03/2018

CONTENTS

Acknowledgments

I thank my parents for my foundation. I thank my brothers for being the first ones to show me what I needed to heal.

I thank the father of my children for three beautiful souls whom I cherish, and who have deepened my journey and shown me the unconditional love I have inside of me.

I thank my clients who have shared their hearts and trusted that they matter.

I thank everyone who helped me with proofreading, editing, and getting my book in print.

I thank you, the reader, for giving me the opportunity to share my life, my experience, and my love.

Thank you for being in my world.

INTRODUCTION

Welcome! My heart's desire is that you find this book helpful. I hope that sharing my experiences in life and in being a therapist help you see that love is the answer to every question—only, always.

When I tell this to people in therapy, it is interesting where their minds go. Some people think I'm crazy, or a love child, or I don't really understand the way the world works. I'm naive, I'm a dreamer, I'm stupid, and I'm unrealistic, to name a few of their labels. They could be right.

Where did your mind go? What decision did you make about me because of this statement? What decision did you make about this book? This is the beginning of your healing through self-awareness. Everyone is on their own journey of healing. It may not look like it; however, everyone is here to heal. What are you here to heal?

The simple and quick answer is whatever shows up in your life: alcoholism, drug addiction, abandonment, fear of success, self-sabotage, self-absorption, or disease. It can also be whatever is in your family: sexual abuse, trauma, neglect, fear, anger, sadness, violence, rape, incest, anorexia, bulimia, grief, illness, aging, loss of function, loss of usefulness, loss of youthfulness, loss of your identify, loss of a loved one, or lack of parenting. These are all different kinds of suffering. You are here to heal that suffering. You are here to heal the suffering in the world—your world. It starts with you.

In the pages to come, may you find a banquet of ideas, suggestions, possibilities, experiences, thoughts served with gentleness, peace, compassion, trust, wonder, and, of course, love.

The majority of this book is written as a conversation. For those of you who love to go to the last chapter of a book to see how it ends, I invite you to do so. The very last chapter, entitled "Shift Happens," reads differently. It is more like a list of sayings that help you shift your thinking in the moment. You can read it to familiarize yourself with the concepts outlined in the book. Or you can read the book as it is written, from chapter 1 to chapter 18. You could also go to (or go back to) the last chapter when it fits for you. You know yourself best; you decide. Ask you.

For those who are interested, I have also written a separate book called *"What Are You Here to Heal? A Self-Reflective Guide."* The guide can be used as a companion on your journey as you deepen your experience of healing. It outlines questions to answer from each chapter and will help you bring to the surface the thoughts that are causing the suffering in your world.

May you feast, indulge, taste, and feel as you try these concepts out for yourself. Be open to questioning your beliefs about yourself and your parents, siblings, family members, spouse, children, coworkers, community, culture and religion. This book is about doing things differently. Being open to seeing things differently.

Enjoy the journey we are all on together. You are not alone. This is what we have come to heal: all the suffering in the world—your world. You just haven't seen it that way before.

CHAPTER 1

Sick and Tired of Being Sick and Tired

Are you sick and tired of being sick and tired? I absolutely love it when people come to therapy and tell me they are sick and tired of being sick and tired. I get very excited. If you are sick and tired of being sick and tired, you are in the best place for change.

It probably doesn't feel like the best place for you to be. When you are sick and tired of being sick and tired, you are usually exhausted, at your wits' end, hopeless, or angry. You often have physical ailments. You may not be able to sleep, eat, or work. Some people say they are sick and tired of being sick and tired, although really they are not—not yet.

The upside to being sick and tired of being sick and tired is that you are usually willing to try something different, something you haven't tried before, or something that is out of your comfort zone. The downside is that you can get stuck there. It is not a nice place to get stuck. You may turn to alcohol, drugs, shopping, gambling, relationships, addiction, and busyness to cope, not realizing that you are distracting yourself from your pain, whether that pain is emotional or physical.

I work in the realm of "you don't know that you don't know." It is like you have tunnel vision. This tunnel is all you can see. It's the only way you see the world, even when there is a whole other world that awaits you. The tunnel vision may persist even when it hurts you.

The good news is that how you "do" life is learned, and it can be unlearned. It can be replaced with something else much more loving to you. If you are sick and tired of being sick and tired, you are stuck. What you have been doing isn't giving you the results that you want: happiness, peace, balance, and love. This is frustrating and can make things appear hopeless.

It is like the way we saw before the invention of the microscope. Before we had microscopes, we couldn't see bacteria, even though bacteria have always been here with us. In fact, bacteria are everywhere—on us and even in us. They have been waiting patiently to be discovered. Microscopes opened a whole new world that has always been with us—we just couldn't see that world before the microscope was developed.

This is what is waiting patiently for you to discover it—a whole new world. Get out your microscope. It gives you new information that will broaden your view, opening your mind and then your heart.

If you are reading this book, you are likely to be willing to open your mind enough to acknowledge that you may not know everything you need to know to be happy and fulfilled. You may be open to possibility. You may have come to the conclusion that you do not know everything. This inquisitive mind-set is your microscope to a whole new world of possibility. It may even be uncomfortable.

I say *uncomfortable* because human beings are invested in being right. This need to be right often stops us from being open to other possibilities, worlds, and realities. It often stops us from truly hearing other people and honoring their points of view. Honoring their points of view doesn't mean you think they are right; it just means you are open to embrace it all, even their opinions.

Can you be comfortable even when someone disagrees with you? Have you noticed how it feels and how you want to defend yourself? Just notice your feelings.

Others are entitled to their opinions. It doesn't mean you have to defend your opinion or attack them for their opinions. If you catch yourself rolling your eyes, you are actually dehumanizing them. If you catch yourself discrediting them or their views, then you are going to war.

Be open enough to let new information into your mind and then into your heart. Be open to others' opinions—and especially to your discomfort. You have been trying to avoid this discomfort for a very long time. Try to be with it and see it for what it is—nothing more, nothing less. If you keep on this journey of self-awareness and healing, you will be able to be with it and come out the other side a more compassionate, loving human being.

When you are sick and tired of being sick and tired, you may be willing to trust yourself enough to trust me enough to try some of the things I suggest. I say *trust yourself* because there is nothing you can't handle.

Have you noticed that despite what you have gone through, you are still standing, even if a little shaken? You may be in the best place to end the suffering in your world. You may be in the best place to ask for what you need, to seek new information, to broaden your perspective, and to get the results that you want.

Are you excited to see this new world? Most people are not excited because they fear the unknown. I am very excited for you. I will hold the space for you until you get excited.

When people are sick and tired of being sick and tired, they are usually very scared. Don't worry. Being scared is what you have been trying to avoid. Stop avoiding it and embrace being scared. You are not crazy. You are normal, and you are not alone. We will just do it together, scared. You are never alone, even when it feels that way to you. Being sick and tired of being sick and tired can be the catalyst you need to further your journey.

For those of you who are not sick and tired of being sick and tired, perhaps you may have a friend who is, or you are just curious. I hope you get what you have come for. In the next pages you will find suggestions, ideas, thoughts, models, and frameworks that may or may not speak to you. Be open to seeing where they fit in your life. Some may fit and others may not. It may look a little different.

For example, you may not steal items from a store; however, you may steal your happiness when you don't let yourself fully be yourself. You may hold yourself back from giving your truth or your opinion, for fear of being wrong or ridiculed. Pulling up your bootstraps and sucking it up may not be working for you. Keep searching until you find out what works for you. Ask you! Be open to see all of you. Don't deny yourself one morsel of healing.

I recommend that you keep a journal to write down your thoughts, ideas, and observations. The greatest journey is into the self. *Who am I? Who do I want to be?* These are the greatest questions you can ask yourself. When you start working with these concepts, you will find intimacy like no other intimacy you have ever known.

You can slow *intimacy* down and think of it like this: in-to-me-see.[1] This is the new frontier. It is so close and appears so far. Like the microscope showing us bacteria, awareness will show you yourself. It has always been there; you just couldn't see it. This new way of looking at yourself and the world is powerful, especially when you are sick and tired of being sick and tired.

I'm so excited for you. Thank you for the honor and privilege of sharing in your journey, our journey together, and everyone's journey.

It has been my experience and the experience of many clients that healing through awareness is your highest truth. It is your greatest journey to a whole new world that is loving, peaceful, generous, compassionate. It is a world full of trust, wonder, freedom, and healing.

CHAPTER 2

Slow Down the Spinning

It has been my experience that when people come for help, they are usually overwhelmed, deeply sad, or even depressed. Life is not working for them. What they usually do to cope is not working for them. They are confused and often completely exhausted.

I call this *spinning*. It is like spinning the wheels of your car when you are stuck: you don't make any progress. Or it can be likened to the spinning you would feel if you were on a hamster wheel or a merry-go-round and you couldn't get off. You are often getting into a deepening predicament with no way out in sight.

If you are doing the same thing over and over again, hoping and expecting a different result, then you are stuck. If you are in an abusive relationship with a parent, partner, friend, child, or coworker, often the only way to stop the spinning is to leave the relationship. It's been my experience that you are holding on to something that isn't worth holding on to. Let go! Letting go doesn't mean you don't care. It just means that you can't do it for someone else. Can you do it for you? That is the real question.

When people are struggling with life's challenges, it is difficult for them to try something different. People often think they are going crazy, or others accuse them of acting crazy. When people leave abusive relationships, they do something that they think is frightening. Only when they have left does it become apparent that they are not crazy, and their minds come back.

I have never worked with anyone whose mind did not come back. Your mind will come back too. Whatever the life challenge is, you are not crazy. When you are living with an abuser, it is very difficult to make sense of what is really going on. You are coping. You are just doing the best you can, getting done what needs to be done: getting up, making breakfast, sending the kids to school, and the whole daily routine.

The busyness of life can often get in the way of seeing what really is going on in your life. This is also multiplied by the number of children you have in your family. You may only need one child to be overwhelmed and some people need five children to get to the place where they are willing to try something different from what they have learned. This hamster wheel, merry go round, putting the left foot in front of the right foot and carrying on, pulling up your boot straps or sucking it up can be so all encompassing and automatic you don't even realize that you are "spinning." You are just doing what needs to be done. The spinning doesn't make sense until you do something different, like leaving the abusive relationship.

The only way I know to stop the spinning is to *heighten your awareness* that you are spinning. I first became aware of this spinning when I was speaking to a friend, telling them what I was up to. My friend said, "You think that's busy?" They proceeded to tell me how busy they were. It felt like a competition. Who is the busiest, who accomplishes the most, who is more exhausted—you get my drift.

Our culture also promotes this busyness. Constant busyness keeps us from becoming consciously present. It keeps us off balance. You are never satisfied. There is always someplace to be or something to do. You are always running, catching up, striving, and exhausted.

Busyness covers a deep emptiness inside human beings. We come to believe that this emptiness is real and can never be filled. It's never enough. We are never enough. Our culture and businesses profit from encouraging this emptiness. You are not tall enough, skinny enough, straight enough, fit enough, young enough, old enough, pretty enough, smart enough, educated enough. Our insatiable consumerism kicks in, telling us a retailer has what you need to make you feel whole, complete, and satisfied. Sellers have products—food, skin-care creams, perfumes, makeup, clothes, homes, cars, and trips. They want you to believe that more stuff will make you happy.

You are being conned. When you get these things, you still won't be happy. Have you noticed? Things will not make you happy.

You were born enough! You just forgot. This is so simple that we often discount it. There is no place to be rather than where you are right now. The past is gone and the future isn't here yet. Your thoughts rob you of the only time you do have: the present. Can you be happy here, in this moment? Now? Your happiness is only a thought away.

Our culture does not support you in that thought. Sellers don't profit if you are happy with your hair, your looks, your weight, your job, your education, your partner, your parents, or your children right now, in this moment.

You are distracted from your true essence. You want happiness and peace. It's available to you every second of every day. You just don't know it or see it yet. It's like the bacteria. Bacteria have always been with us. We just couldn't see them until we had the microscope. You have always been enough. You couldn't see it. It is especially hard to see when businesses profit from our fears and when our egos are running our lives.

Fill in the blank: I will be happy when—

When will you be happy? Maybe you said, "I'll be happy when I pay off my student loans." I'm not saying don't pay off your student loans. I'm not saying don't get an education. I'm in the education business. I'm saying be happy with your student loans. There is no better investment than investing in you. Be happy paying off your student loans. That is what taking 100 percent responsibility for your life looks like. Don't wait until your loans are all paid off to be happy. Often when people *do* pay off their student loans, they still are not happy. Something else has taken the loans' place as the thing they need to make them happy.

Be happy here, now, in the present, not sometime in the future. Your happiness is your choice.

When you argue with what is, you lose. When you want a thing to be something that it isn't, that desire is painful. Suffering is your choice. You cannot change what has already happened. However, you can change your response.

Depression occurs when you want something to be different than what it is.[2]

I want my father to show up for me. I want my mom to forgive me. I want my children to respect me. I want my employer to appreciate me. I want my coworker to understand me. I want my parents to listen to me. When you want another person to do something, and they don't, notice that you have made your happiness depend on them.

When you believe someone shouldn't have died and they did, you are arguing with reality. When you think something shouldn't have happened and it did, you are arguing with what is. I'm not saying that "what is" is right. I'm saying you can't change it, and you wanting something to be different than what is only makes you suffer.

I'm not saying don't grieve. Grieving is normal and necessary. There comes a time of acceptance of what you can't change. Sometimes we think how long we grieve is a measure of how much we love. If we love, then we have to suffer. It's important to heighten your awareness and question your thoughts. If I move on and accept loss, does it mean I didn't love the person I lost?

Look at what you are thinking. What thoughts are running your life? Make a list. Heighten your awareness. Most people don't know the thoughts that are running their lives.

When you come to the realization that you have a choice, a light bulb goes on. There is a shift. You are not a robot or a zombie repeating a familiar pattern. Events do not get to define who you are.

For example, sometimes people who have been raped think they are "damaged goods." Often they replay the rape over and over in their minds. Part of this is the healing process and is very normal. Most sufferers don't know it is normal. Unfortunately, sometimes people get stuck and are unable to rebuild their lives. This is not helpful or loving.

Finish the following sentences, filling in the blanks as you would for yourself or to show how you feel about others in that situation:

I was abandoned, and this means _____.

I am divorced, and this means _____.

I was conceived before wedlock,
and this means _____.

I was neglected as a child, and this means _____.

I was raped, and this means _____.

I was sexually abused by _____,
and this means _____.

I was _____,
and this means _____.

Challenge every belief you have that is critical, disturbing, or unhelpful. Challenge anything that makes you angry or keeps you spinning. Question what happened to you and what you make it mean. Question your circumstances, your culture, your gender, yourself.

Have you noticed that very few people like their hair color or type of hair? If they have straight hair, they want curly hair. If they have curly hair, they want straight hair. Slow down the spinning enough to see what thoughts are running your life.

One thought can keep you in an abusive relationship.

"But I love them, so I can't leave."

"It's my father. It's my mother. I can't leave them."

"I can't leave my partner. I made a commitment: till death do us part."

"We have children together. I can't forsake them."

"My parents were divorced, and I don't want that for my children."

The form is different but the content is the same.[3] Your repeated unquestioned thoughts keep you suffering. They are running your life.

Do your circumstances, sex, skin color, or education get to define you? What kind of person do you want to be? Is this image in your mind in alignment with who you are?

I want to be loving, peaceful, fulfilled, and happy. What would that look like? Write it in your journal. You get to decide. You get to define you for you. Ask you. This is true power.

This is not what our consumerist society wants. You are much easier to control and manipulate when you are suffering and feeling inadequate. When suffering, you are more likely to buy stuff, get high, or abuse people to fill your perceived emptiness.

Slow down the spinning enough to ask yourself who and what gets to define you. Who benefits if I stay in this state? Is this who I want to be? Raise your awareness of the thoughts that are running your life. If you are having trouble, ask someone to help you—a friend, a colleague, or a loved one.

Listen to your child. Children have amazing insights if you are willing to listen. My five-year-old once asked me, "Why are you upset, Mommy?"

I quickly answered, "Oh, I'm not upset, sweetheart."

In two minutes, I was very upset. My five-year-old child knew I was upset before I knew I was upset. This was a huge lesson for me. Others often know you better than you think. It is important to ask for help from those you respect and be open to their answers and suggestions.

I would like to mention briefly some other ways that clients have found helpful to slow down the spinning. It is important that you keep looking for what works for you. There are many good books, CDs, and classes on mindfulness, anchoring, meditation, yoga, breath work, tai chi, laughter, hobbies, volunteering, music, and creative expression. Being in nature is another great way you can slow down the spinning in your life. Nothing makes you more present than acknowledging the majestic beauty of a sunset, a flock of geese in flight, a heron standing in a marsh, or a fish jumping out of the water.

Slowing down the spinning, calming yourself, and heightening your awareness of what is really going on in your life are the first steps that work. You can do this.

Don't be surprised if you collapse. I can remember not wanting to sit down, because if I sat down, I would fall asleep. I was physically and emotionally exhausted. I had to slow down the spinning. Doing more of what I was doing was not working. It's about doing it differently. Start by slowing down the spinning.

CHAPTER 3

Six Traps of the Ego

Once you start noticing what thoughts are running your life, it is helpful to identify the traps of the ego. I have a very simple way of defining the ego. The ego is the voice inside your head that keeps you small and suffering. I have found that the ego disguises itself very well. The ego has six major traps:

1. Trying to understand things
2. Unrealistic expectations
3. Should and shouldn't
4. Extreme or excess of anything
5. Confusion
6. Comparing

Sometimes the ego spends most of its time in one kind of trap. Other times it tag teams with other thought-traps. It's the ego's way of keeping you off balance, so you don't understand what is actually happening and actually running your life.

For example, a person can get stuck trying to figure out why something happened.

"Why were they spared when everyone else died?"

"Why did lightning strike me?"

"What did I do wrong?"

"Why would someone do something like that?"

You can spend hours, days, months, or even years trying to figure out a situation. Figure out one kind of trap, and the ego often moves on to another kind of trap. In this way, the ego keeps you in a constant state of suffering.

Generally, the ego doesn't want you to suffer so much that you will commit suicide, because it would die too. Your ego doesn't want to die. However, it does want to stay in charge of your life. The ego wants to make you suffer just enough to make you easy to control.

Generally, people who are suicidal are very ambivalent. Most suicidal thoughts don't end in suicide. More often than not, suicide attempts are calls for help. They fail or are thwarted. Most suicidal individuals want the pain in their heads, hearts, or bodies to stop. They often feel they are a burden to family and friends.

You think the voice in your head is you. It is not. You are the observer listening to the voice in your head. This may appear to be a very strange concept at first, however try it. Listen to the constant chatter in your head. Your ego never shuts up. Have you noticed? This is especially true when you are sick and tired of being sick and tired. The ego is so loud and in charge that you can't sleep. Your mind is spinning. Another time when the ego is particularly loud is when you are driving your car.

Just notice. Write down when you notice you are suffering and what you are thinking about. Heighten your awareness of what your ego is telling you. Listen for the six major traps of the ego. Are you stuck in one trap? Do you have the tag team going on? I often say that each person has a top two or three traps, and just when you think you have them handled, your ego changes it up and throws another kind at you. This keeps you from seeing the pattern. You never quite put your finger on what is going on. You often default to an overwhelmed state, which leads back to spinning. The ego is very ingenious.

The first trap is *trying to understand things*. Our culture loves to figure things out, analyze, pick apart, compartmentalize, and solve problems. We are taught critical thinking skills and project management. We break projects down into manageable pieces. Science is based on trying to understand things. This is, generally speaking, a wonderful skill. However, when you are experiencing intense life challenges, this approach can backfire into a trap, especially when what you are thinking about doesn't make sense.

For example, why would anyone intentionally hurt another human being? Well, I could give you lots of suggestions, and in the final analysis, it may not matter to your peace. You get stuck in the explanation, trapped in trying to figure it out. Why did the attacker do that? If only someone had intervened, said this, done that. The constant attempts to understand why can make you feel like you are crazy.

Some situations and actions literally do not make any sense. If you notice that you are stuck trying to understand things, just know that your ego is running your life. Skip the explanation. It may or may not make any sense at this time. Stop, and be happy from here. If you are stuck figuring things out, it will bring you no peace.

In fact, I have found that being right is pretty empty. So what? You are right. You figured it out or you think you have understood the situation. Do you want to be right, or do you want to be happy? If you still want to be right, what is the cost? I invite you to choose happiness over being right every time.

Some people get caught in what I call "double dipping." This is when, no matter what they think, they are confused or unhappy. Either option keeps you spinning. For example, you have a decision to make. You have two choices, A and B. Neither choice will make every person affected by your decision happy. If you choose A, which is what you want, you will feel guilty. If you choose B, then others will be happy, although the outcome is not what you want. That is double dipping.

Again, just stop and notice. No matter what you choose or think you are suffering, notice how trapped you are when you are double dipping. It's the perfect dilemma. No matter what you do, you are going to disappoint someone. Are you going to disappoint others or yourself?

The second trap is *unrealistic expectations*. It's unrealistic that I expect to complete a complex task in fifteen minutes. It is unrealistic that I expect my child to have teeth at three months. It is unrealistic to expect another person to read my mind. We have many unrealistic expectations of ourselves and of others.

There are, additionally, unrealistic expectations that others may have of you. For example, it may be unrealistic of your partner to expect you to work full-time, make dinner, clean up, and get the children bathed and put to bed. We often don't realize that these unrealistic expectations are running our lives.

It's unrealistic to be all things to your partner. It's unrealistic to expect someone to be grateful when they are not. It's unrealistic to think that people don't lie sometimes. Have you ever lied? If you are (basically) honest, you will see that we have all lied at least once.

Find your unrealistic expectations. Explore them. Usually expectations come from patterns—our desire to predict the world and how we want things to be. Just notice what unrealistic expectations are running your life. Write them down.

The third trap is shoulds and shouldn'ts. This is similar to the second trap, nevertheless deserves its own category.

"I should be married by now."

"I should have known!"

"I should have done better on that exam."

"I shouldn't have done that."

"You should do this and then I'll be happy."

"I know what you should do."

Does anyone really know what another human being should or shouldn't do? Your ego will tell you yes, that you should know what another human being should or shouldn't do. But should and shouldn't bring you no peace. They only bring you suffering.

Don't get in the spot where you *shouldn't* be kind or stick up for yourself or be caring. You will be double dipping again. Slow down the spinning enough to notice when you say *should* and *shouldn't*. You will catch yourself if you are looking.

The fourth trap of the ego is an *extreme or excess of anything*. If someone calls you four times, that is excess. If you drink until you drop, that is excess. If you do the same thing over and over again, expecting a different response, that is excess. We often get stuck in these patterns and don't realize it unless we slow the spinning down enough to see it.

Look at the excess in your life. What are you doing over and over again? Write it down. Are you choosing partners who abuse you? Are you transferring your addiction from one thing to another? Are you thinking the same thoughts over and over again? Notice. Take the time to see what thoughts are running your life. You will be amazed at what you will find.

I had a client whose partner would text six times during a group session. The partner did this despite where the client was and that they were unable to answer. The client stated that it was easier to text back than to deal with the fallout of not responding. I identified this as an example of excess. The texts were distracting to the person receiving the texts and disrespectful to the whole group. Texts often masquerade as attentiveness, caring, or thoughtfulness. In this case, the texts made an excellent example of abusive and controlling behavior.

The fifth trap of the ego is *confusion*. The ego loves confusion. If you are confused, then your ego is running your life. It's that simple. We make it very complicated. What should I do? What shouldn't I do?

Did you catch the *should* and *shouldn't*? Keep noticing.

My personal favorite: What's my purpose? What am I supposed to do with my life? I don't know what to do!

That's right—you don't know what to do! You make the best decision you can at the time. That is all any of us can do. You can't do it wrong.

However, your ego will tell you that you did do it wrong. Well, what if you make a decision and it is wrong? You clean up your mess, and you go on from there, having learned what not to do. These are not mistakes. These are opportunities to learn.

Your ego will give you no rest. Have you noticed? You don't get to be human. You have to be perfect or tragically defective. Either end of the continuum and every point in between will bring you no peace. Perfection is sterile, empty, and lonely. Tragically defective is lost, destructive, and hopeless. Either way, the ego is running your life. You are suffering.

Just notice when your ego is running your life. Where is your mind? Where are your thoughts? If you are confused, then your ego is running your life. It's that simple. Just notice. Catch yourself when you are confused and write it down. Put the confusion on paper and look at it with new awareness.

The last trap of the ego is *comparing* yourself to others. This may seem unassuming, however so much is tied up in competitiveness, especially within families. For example, I had a client whose parent would often compare the client to a cousin. The client felt they could never live up to their cousin's achievements and was resentful.

Has anyone ever said to you, "You're not living up to your potential"? This is a subtle and often unconscious type of comparing. It's said to encourage you. Unfortunately, very few people ever feel encouraged. Rather, they feel judged. They are missing the mark or not doing enough.

Don't get me wrong. I'm not saying don't be competitive, in the sense of being active or staying fit. I enjoy organized sports. However, when competition warps perception and people don't feel their skills are good enough to allow them to participate, that's when confusion runs rampant.

Competitiveness has many forms, which adds to the confusion. There is the competitiveness that encourages you to work harder, practice, and win scholarships. These are examples of good competition. There is also hurtful competition, such as hazing, discrimination, prejudice, bigotry, intolerance, and every "ism" you can think of.

To raise your awareness, your task is catching the ego when it is using a trap. This helps to create distance between you and your ego. You are not your ego. You are the one listening to your ego. You get to choose whether you are going to listen and get totally absorbed in the constant chatter. Or you can choose to see that the chatter is not you.

Seeing the ego takes practice, like strengthening a muscle. This is a very empowering practice. Slowing down the spinning helps you identify the traps and see that you are not the chatter in your head. You don't have to believe everything you think. In fact, I would encourage you *not* to believe everything you think. Just notice what you are thinking. Thought comes before feelings and action.

If you are stuck in any of the six traps I have described, then your ego is running your life. Stop. Notice. Work at catching when your mind goes there. Write down your observations and concerns. This is the beginning of the end of your suffering.

I find it helpful to use an analogy about fishing and the kinds of bait that are used to catch a fish. Your ego wants to bait the big one. Oh, that's you! You're the big one. You are the fish. Your ego gets the fishing pole and fishing line. It gets a weight, a bobber, and a tackle box. Then it tries a worm for bait—one of the six traps. A worm works most of the time. You are trapped spinning, and your ego is happy. Sometimes worms don't keep you spinning enough, so your ego tries minnows. Ah, minnows. Yeah, a different kind of trap gets you spinning a little faster. Next might come a flashy new lure. You know, one with bright colors, a shiny hook, and the most exquisite shape. Before you know it, you are spinning so much that you can't sleep. Your mind is racing.

Sound familiar? The form is different, but the content is the same. You are spinning. Just notice. Notice what kind of trap is keeping you spinning right now. Write it down. Get it on paper. Look at it. Get it out of your head. It is easier to see when it's on paper. Writing it down creates a bit of distance between your thoughts, who you think you are, who you want to be, and your ego.

You get to choose who you want to be. What I am asking you to do may make you feel uncomfortable at first. I could make a hefty bet that before now, you haven't looked at yourself as a fish to be caught by your ego. This is what it looks like to start taking 100 percent responsibility for your life. This is really good news. This is something you can do. You don't have to wait for anyone. Who do you want to be? Ask you. Write it down on paper.

Often people talk about killing the ego or making peace with the ego. My experience is that you can't kill your ego or make peace with it. You can only see the ego for what it is and not let it run your life. Awareness is the only successful way I know to manage the ego.

Notice when you are suffering. Notice which trap the ego is using to keep you suffering. It can be a low-grade suffering, or you can be sick and tired of being sick and tired. Write down your ego's favorite traps. The ego may be on overdrive and using all six traps. Perhaps it has been running your life for so long that you are out of control and can't tell the difference between yourself and your ego.

Notice and identify the types of trap. I can hear my ego saying, "You have just asked your readers to *understand* their ego, which is one of the traps. So you are using a trap to understand what you are trying to get them to understand. You know that is confusing—which, by the way, is another trap. So now you are double dipping. No, actually you are triple dipping."

What is your ego saying? Write it down. Notice how you feel. Get your power back. Noticing that you are not your ego and challenging your thoughts can be empowering. It can feel like you are shining a light in a dark room. There can be acceptance and an absence of fear.

I'm not saying I have all the answers. I do know when my ego is loud and trying to take charge of my life through suffering thoughts. When is your ego loud and when is it taking charge of your life? Write it down and notice how it feels. Choose to be the listener and the observer. Come back to who you want to be in this moment. Ask you.

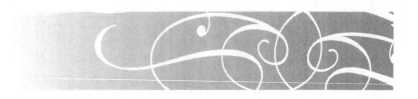

CHAPTER 4

Discernment

So how do I know when my ego is running my life? I call this *discernment*, the ability to look at things differently, with new knowledge and awareness. It may seem confusing at first. Use your discernment.

Let me say that again. If you are confused, then your ego is running your life. So how do you discern?

I like to keep things simple and easy to follow. The first step is to slow down the spinning so you can question and identify your thoughts. Things really are not that complicated. How do you know you are "supposed" to be reading this book? You read this book. How do you know you are not "supposed" to read this book? You don't. It's that simple.

We make things very complicated. "Oh, you should read this book. It could help you!" That is one of the six traps of the ego. There is a "should" in that sentence. Did you catch it? Practice! Practice! Practice!

Heighten your awareness enough to see what is running your life. Look to see where the six traps of the ego are running your life. You get to decide who you want running your life. It is you or your ego?

This is 100 percent responsibility for your life. Some may not like that idea. However, it is the only thing I have found that works in my life and in the life of every client I have ever worked with on the path of self-discovery and healing. This is especially true if you are sick and tired of being sick and tired. Taking responsibility is for the bold and brave. There is no quick fix, pill, salve, or ointment that makes your suffering go away. You are it!

That is actually good news. You may not think so at first. When you start working with these concepts, your freedom depends on opening your mind to these concepts. Test them out for yourself. Ask you. Someone else cannot make you happy. A thing cannot make you happy.

A person or thing may make you feel happy at first because you think you are getting what you want. If getting what you want actually leaves you feeling empty, notice. If you are still unhappy when you get what you want, notice. You are asking someone or something else to fill the emptiness in you that can't be filled by anyone except you.

Notice how you feel and use discernment. You do not have to wait for a person you love to change. You do not have to just love them when they do what you want them to do. That is called *conditional love*. "I'll love you when you do what I want."

Your happiness doesn't depend on anyone or anything except you. "No one gets to ruin my life; that's my job." I know it is a bit of a mind stretch, and it may feel uncomfortable. Grapple with these concepts and try them out for yourself. Ask you! You are the key. It's not so much what happens to you rather what you make it mean.

If something happens that, I feel, was bad, what do I make it mean? "I asked for it; it's my fault; I deserved it; I was in the wrong place at the wrong time; why would anyone do that to me?" When you ask those questions, what are you telling yourself? Are you replaying the event over and over in your head? Your thoughts may become triggered by smells, places, tastes, or objects. Write them down. Did the event happen once, twice, five times, ten times? Did you play it over and over in your mind thousands of times? Maybe you can't sleep. Maybe you can't eat. Shine a light on what you are thinking and feeling. In-to-me-see. Just notice.

Thought comes before feeling. You may not think so at first. Try this concept out: notice. We often believe feelings come first. Slow down the spinning to see for yourself what comes first. Question, explore, and discern your experience. Ask you. Notice.

This may not be for everyone. Try it out for you. If it sounds like a different version of "pull yourself up by your bootstraps" or "suck it up," look again. See what is really there, masquerading as defensiveness, insecurity, justification, and punishment. This is a deeper conversation about you and how you discern.

CHAPTER 5

The Car of Your Life

Another way to look at discernment is to use a metaphor. Who is driving the car of your life? Is your ego driving the car, or are you? Who are you and who is it you want to be?

It may be helpful to think of "you" as the driver, with "you" being your higher or highest self. If you are comfortable with the terminology of faith, you can articulate this as your soul driving the car of your life. I am not invested in what word you use; I encourage you to find out what fits for you. You get to choose. Be open to using different words for a while and find out what fits for you. You might feel more comfortable defining "you" as love. That fits with what I stated earlier: love is the answer to every question.

Okay, okay, I know I went someplace you may not have seen coming. And you may not be ready for it. However, now is the time. You have gone this far; you might as well keep reading.

It is important for you to discern and choose whether you or your ego is going to drive the car of your life. What fits for you? Try things and see. Be open to embrace all. You can change your mind too.

I will never ask you to do or say anything illegal, immoral, or life-threatening. If I or anyone else asks you to do such things, they are frauds and you need to get yourself somewhere safe.

I hope I have encouraged you to say your truth and explore what you think. I hope you will try some of these concepts.

We are all connected through our souls, egos, journey, healing, challenges, and love. We are more alike than we are different. This is that 100 percent responsibility thing again.

I love the car metaphor for two reasons. First, most people can relate to who is driving a car. Second, most cars have a trunk or a backseat. You can never get rid of your ego; however, you can put it in the trunk or the backseat and not let it drive. I joke that you can banish your ego to the roof of your car. You won't even need to tie it, because it will hold on for dear life.

If the ego is not going to let go of you, can you let go of it? Your ego wants to drive the car of your life, especially if you are spinning.

The ego does have a good function: it usually lets you know about dangers, internal and external. It just goes into overdrive sometimes, and you get stuck there without realizing that you are stuck. This is about discerning when your ego is running your life. Sometimes you can just put your ego in the trunk of the car. Sometimes your ego looks like a dear friend who is part of the very fabric of your life. Sometimes your ego is about acknowledging the not-so-pretty sides of ourselves, such as jealousy, pettiness and insecurity. This journey is about acknowledging all parts of ourselves, even our egos. It is very inclusive.

As long as your ego is not driving the car of your life, you are going to be okay. This is a different paradigm. It is about living in the world and driving the car of your life yourself. By letting "you" drive your car, you are being true to yourself. You are living a healed life in which love is the answer to every question—love for you and love for others. There is healing through learning, growth, development, creativity, acceptance, problem solving, spontaneity, trust, and wonder.

If you are sick and tired of being sick and tired, then your ego has been running your life. Your higher self, deeper awareness, or soul is patiently waiting for you to wake up. Just like the bacteria waiting to be seen through a microscope, you are waiting for your deeper meaning and healing to be discovered. "You" are like the bacteria in this analogy. That higher self has always been there; you just didn't notice it or honor yourself in that way. "You" are the one you have been waiting for all your life.

Unless you question your thoughts or use your microscope, you may never grapple with understanding yourself. There have probably been many wake-up calls along the way. You have not noticed or you didn't understand their purpose. Perhaps you doubted whether they were really wake-up calls.

For example, you may "get the feeling" that someone can't be trusted. Even so, you ignored the feeling and trusted them anyway. Then you ended up getting hurt. So the next time you have that feeling, you can ignore it again, or you can listen and make a different choice.

If you ignore the wake-up calls, just notice that your life will get louder and louder, which means it will spin even *more*. You will feel like you have been here before, that this is the same or perhaps a little worse. If you keep ignoring yourself, the discomfort will continue to increase.

Perhaps a physical example will help. You are not feeling well, and you don't seek medical attention. You are still managing to go to work, eat, and do life. The symptoms continue to get worse. Then they go away for a day once you stay at home and rest. Wow! You are feeling better. Awesome. You go back to work—only to be rushed to the hospital. There were wake-up calls all along the way; you just ignored them. If you continue to ignore the wake-up calls, they will get louder. Often they get so loud, you can't ignore them anymore.

Another example is when you look at your relationships and notice that all of your partners have been abusive. They may have been abusive differently or to a greater or lesser extent; however, they have all been abusive. Often, once your partner leaves, your children get more abusive. You may notice that some of your friends are abusive too. A pattern emerges. You think, "What is it about me that I'm attracting only abusive people in my life?" I love it when people ask themselves this question. This is when I know a client is becoming conscious of their thoughts, patterns, and situation.

Perhaps you have left a partner for a new relationship. Then that new person doesn't satisfy you, and you leave for yet another person. Four or five relationships down this road, you are still not happy. Just notice. You may wake up and come to the conclusion, "Maybe it's me?" This doesn't mean that you can't date several people; it just means that there may be a pattern. Or perhaps you are double dipping. It doesn't matter what you think or who you are with; you are unhappy. You are the only one who can discern for you. You are the only person who can make you happy. That is what discernment is about.

Another example is when you realize you are addicted to your hurts. You have confused hurt with love. This is particularly confusing for people who have been sexually abused by a parent, relative, or family friend. They often still love their abusers after all the things the abusers have done. It has been my experience that it is never wrong to love someone, even if that person has hurt you. It is important to stop an abuser from hurting you again, however it doesn't mean you have to stop loving them. I encourage you to acknowledge your confusion and love from a place of loving yourself more. Love is the answer to every question. Love just might look a little different. Opening your mind will open your heart.

It is often not until you land in the hospital or can't sleep, eat, or work that you understand that what you are doing is not working for you. You may notice the natural addictions, such as food, sex, or power, or the unnatural addictions, such as drugs, gambling, religion, and money. If you have full-blown addictions, your life has not been working for you for a while—you just didn't know what to do about it.

Now you know what to do: acknowledge that what you are doing isn't working. Perhaps you have even used the words "I'm sick and tired of being sick and tired." Slow down the spinning enough to see the thoughts that are running your life. Identify your ego traps. Practice discernment. Look at things differently. Take 100 percent responsibility for your life. Put your ego in the trunk of the car of your life.

Now you know. You can't go back to unconsciousness. You are changing. You can do this because I have seen hundreds of people do it. You are designed to heal. This practice is healing. We all come to acknowledge our true essence and nature. Your love is the answer to every question. You just didn't know it until now. It is healing. This is what it looks like to take 100 percent responsibility for your life.

If you have hung in this long and practiced heightening your awareness, there is no going back. There is nothing to go back to. You won't want anything less than your true identity. Welcome to the beginning of a new paradigm.

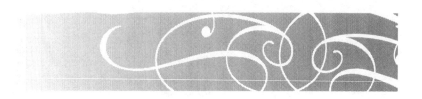

CHAPTER 6

The Accordion of Life

Your ego will tell you that you haven't made any progress. It will tell you that you are deluding yourself, you can't change, you can't be truly happy. Can you hear your ego? Well, are you going to listen to your ego or to you? *Who do you want to listen to?*

You can tell you that your birthright is peace. You can trust yourself. You are not alone. You can be happy. You just have to decide whom you choose to believe.

This may sound very simplistic, and you are right. It is very simple to make a choice. You are your choices. We make choices all the time. Even when you don't make a choice, you are making a choice. How simple is that? It is truly amazing. Just notice.

It is not so much what happens to you; rather, it is what you make it mean. You can't change what happened to you. You can change what you make it mean. You have been choosing your ego and fear for a very long time. The fact that you are still searching means that somewhere inside of you, you know there is a better way. You tap in and achieve some inner knowing where, secretly and deeply, you want there to be another way.

Your ego wants you to keep spinning so you never find another way. Your ego never wants you to find peace, because if you find peace, the ego believes it won't have a purpose and will die. The ego doesn't want to die. This is why the ego keeps you spinning.

This is about liberating your ego with a new awareness of the thought system that has always been with us. We were born with it. Your ego doesn't have to keep you spinning anymore if you find peace, joy, compassion, contentment, and your true identity. Liberating your ego means acknowledging and honoring that part of you and bringing all of you with you on your journey. Your peace is undeniably a thought away. Your power is choosing what thought is going to run your life. Your healing is in your mind. When you change your mind, you change your world.

Your ego will tell you, if you try these concepts, that you really haven't made any changes, or that the concepts are psychobabble, too simple, or too hard. Your ego will tell you whatever works to maintain the status quo of your suffering.

If you look more deeply, you will find that life is like playing an accordion. You are making music every time you believe in your truth and your higher self. You are making progress in the same way an accordion makes music. You will go in and out, however you will never go back to where you started. You have been forever changed by picking up the accordion and playing the instrument of your life. You will be forever changed by taking 100 percent responsibility for how and what you think.

Your ego will tell you, "You haven't made any progress. Everything is the same. You are still suffering." This often happens to people in recovery. They feel now that they are "clean," "drug free," or "recovered," and therefore life should be wonderful and stress-free.

There are two traps of the ego in that statement: *should* and *unrealistic expectations*. Did you notice?

It's unrealistic to believe that life will not have any challenges once you have tried something different. Life will always have challenges. That is not going to change. You still have to pay your bills. You still have unexpected events. You still have unpredictability. It's how you meet those challenges and what you make the challenges mean that has changed.

That is the in and out of the accordion of your life or the up and downs of life. You can put the accordion down; however, you can't go back. There is no "back" to go back to. The past is over. You made music. You have had a taste of another way to do life. You are forever changed.

Stay present. Stay with your awareness in this moment: now, now, now. This is where your power is, in this moment. Your ego will tell you that you have gone right back to where you were. You haven't gone back. It is slightly different, and you have a different awareness.

There will always be challenges. You get to choose how you meet those challenges. You may be choosing suffering thoughts, like "nothing has changed," "I'm back where I started," and "I'm still suffering." Just notice. Your ego is fighting for its life when it gives you these messages. Notice your ego. Acknowledge it. Let it come out of the dark shadows. It can't hurt you when you see it for what it is and accept that it has a role. Its role is to show you what still needs to be healed. Work on the healing. Then other thoughts may start appearing, like "everything is changing," "I can't ever go back to where I started," and "I don't have to suffer."

It has been my experience that you cannot kill your ego. I recommend that you not try. It is futile. If you kill your ego, you kill a part of yourself. It is not bad and wrong to have an ego. It has a healthy function, just like having a conscience. Bring your ego with you. Embrace that human side of you and laugh.

It is just that the ego is in overdrive when you are sick and tired of being sick and tired. Put the ego in the trunk of the car of your life. Look at the thoughts. Don't let your ego drive. Keep noticing the suffering thoughts. Notice when "you" are driving and when the ego is driving.

Practice. Practice. Practice. Practice slowing down the spinning to notice that thought comes before feeling. Enjoy the music of the accordion of your life. No one can stop the in and out or ups and downs. You can choose how you respond to them. Just notice.

CHAPTER 7

Being Human

I didn't know when I was growing up how I loathed the fragility and the limited parameters of being human. I didn't appreciate my frailty or that this body has to die eventually. I couldn't do certain things because of my size, my gender, my lot in life, and my age.

Human beings are delicate, not perfect. We have limits (mostly self-imposed) and we don't even know it. We have insecurities, fears, compulsions, desires, and hormones, just to name a few. We have been known to lie, cheat, steal, plot, scheme, sabotage, and project our stuff onto others so we never take responsibility for our own stuff.

What I am proposing is exactly the opposite. We are 100 percent responsible for what we think, no matter the circumstances. This is where your power lies, in taking responsibility.

Note that I didn't say take 100 percent responsibility for the circumstances. I said to take 100 percent responsibility for what you *think*, no matter the circumstance. See reality the way it is, not the way you think it should be.

Did you catch the *should*? Just checking! Keep your sense of humor.

It amazes me that people are so shocked to learn that someone is an addict. Of course we are addicts. We are hard-wired to be addicts. It's surprising there are not more addicts. When we are growing up, children thrive on consistency, predictability, and attachment to the adults in their lives. We eat three times a day. We get up every day, sleep every day and eliminate waste every day.

We also start off completely helpless and dependent on our caregivers to give us what we need. Some caregivers are better than others. Some are awesome, and some are just doing the best they can.

How do we get our needs met? How do we let people know what we need? Of course we are addicts. It's especially the case if we have experienced physical or emotional abandonment, neglect, or abuse.

If you were raised by an alcoholic, workaholic, or drug-addicted parent, then your parent was significantly unavailable to you. If you were hungry or left alone for long periods of time, then you were neglected. If one or both of your parents were overly critical, dominating, controlling, or possessive, you were emotionally abused. If you witnessed someone being emotionally, physically, or sexually abused, then you were also emotionally, physically, or sexually abused. You were not able to stop or get away from the abuse.

Any of these situations and hundreds of others can cause profound insecurity, fear, jealousy, loneliness, possessiveness, and addiction.

We are all addicts sometimes in our lives, especially when we face challenges. We often look to our habits and routines to help us cope. We do more, faster, better, and longer in an attempt to get the result that we want. We may start with small things to help us feel more accepted by others. Then we may sell out on ourselves for the fear of offending a loved one. Our circumstances may change—an injury, a loss, a natural disaster—and precipitate an addictive cycle.

For example, in my twenties, I was hit by a car. I had been riding my bicycle, and I thought, "It is dusk, and I am wearing dark-blue clothes. I am about to enter one of the busiest intersections in town. A hill is coming up that makes it very difficult for drivers to see." I listened to these internal warnings, got off my bike, and walked it through the pedestrian crosswalk.

A car hit me anyway.

I wasn't hurt very badly. I was knocked to the ground on top of my bike. I was so afraid of being run over on the ground that I threw my bike and myself out of the intersection.

I was eventually taken to the hospital. I had to walk on crutches afterward, though fortunately no limbs were broken. I couldn't dance at my parents' twenty-fifth wedding anniversary that I had been planning as a surprise for about six months. I was at university, working on my master's degree in social work, and not one person asked me how I was or what had happened. I found this particularly odd. Social work is supposed to be a caring profession, right? I would get really teary or start crying for no reason at all. I realized that I was grieving the loss of the function of my leg. It really rocked everything I was doing and had planned.

Sometimes the best of intentions and every plan we make to keep ourselves safe get thrown out the window. We just can't plan for every contingency.

I did get better. I put on a brave face and sat through my classes and my parents' anniversary party. Unfortunately, I felt robbed, victimized, and misunderstood. Others seemed unsympathetic to my situation.

Does this sound familiar? You can't change the circumstances. You can change your thinking about the circumstances. When things happen our way, we believe that we are in control. In reality, it is pure grace. It has nothing to do with us. It is pure grace that anything happens the way we think it should happen.

Was I *supposed to be* hit by a car? It happened. There are two components at work here. First, there's the need to acknowledge that it happened and I couldn't change it. Second, there's what I made it mean.

Initially, I made it mean that I should have prevented the accident from happening and I didn't. That's magical thinking. Something *shouldn't* have happened? Did you catch that? I also made the situation mean that people didn't notice or care about me. I felt disappointed and sad. They should have noticed and been polite enough to ask me what happened. Did you notice the *should*? Keep noticing the *shoulds* and *shouldn'ts* in your life. Write them down. Look at them, see them for what they are, traps of the ego and get free.

Generally, people try to deaden their physical and emotional pain, especially their painful feelings. We seem to have so many overwhelming feelings such as nervous, bored, irritated, excited, horrified, disgusted, inspired, lonely, hurt and foolish to name a few.

The ego loves confusion, and there are many words to describe how we feel. For simplicity's sake, you are either happy or not happy, suffering or not suffering.

We often hide a very deep feeling of sad and mad with alcohol, food, shopping, gambling, exercise, sex, relationships, or work to avoid the physical and mental pain in our lives. This is where the spinning gets started. We are afraid to feel the depth and intensity of feelings. We are all addicts sometimes.

This avoidance of suffering—physical, psychological, or emotional pain—is the basis of our addictions. We don't want to feel bad, sad, mad, scared or fear. Our addictions help us not to feel these feelings. Addictions distract us from feeling our feelings. Our addictions numb us even to happiness, if we are willing to notice. We are known to sometimes self-sabotage our happiness. We don't feel worthy of being truly happy. We don't feel worthy of being loved. This is the double dipping I was talking about earlier.

It has been my experience and the experience of hundreds of my clients that you can walk through these feelings, experience what you are trying to avoid, and come out healed and happy. You may say, "That's easy for you to say." It has been my experience. Try it out for yourself.

The fear in your head is actually much worse than reality. Just notice. I have walked many people through their fears triumphantly. You need to trust yourself and then me. Try these concepts out for yourself. Notice. Keep noticing. Write down your fears, patterns, ego traps, and choice of addictions. Notice when you want to lie, when you get uncomfortable, when you don't ask for what you need. Look at the reasons you tell yourself to justify what you think. Look at what you do when you are uncomfortable. See what is there.

In-to-me-see. This is intimacy with yourself, looking at what you are trying to hide from others and even yourself. These are the deep wounds that we carry. It is time to let go of them and expose the sadness. Bring your sadness and suffering up to heal. Write down what is there for you. There is nothing there that you cannot heal. This is very exciting in my world. Embrace your fear, supported and loved.

I have worked in domestic violence for over twenty years. People ask me all the time, "That must be so hard—how do you do it?" It hasn't always been easy. I left once, only to realize I came back to heal. The first time, I wanted people to like me. I was a supervisor and I was a good person. I was a good supervisor and a good employee. It didn't matter. It didn't make people like me or be happy. The only thing I could change was how I thought. I couldn't change them.

I took everything very personally. It was a chaotic time at my workplace, moving from one location to another. Staff had never had another supervisor; they'd had direct access to the executive director. The agency was experiencing normal growing pains. At the time, I was getting bogus emergency calls at home, dealing with irritable staff. These challenges were leaving me with deeper and deeper sadness. Nothing ever seemed like it was getting resolved. The staff were unhappy, bitter, and very toxic. I had also become pregnant with my second child. My mother had died just two years prior, and we had moved to a brand-new city. Life was getting overwhelming really quickly. Oh, did I mention that I was a perfectionist?

I chose to heal my life and my thinking—or, more accurately, life changed me.

When I came back to work in domestic violence, I had already started working on me. Life gave me lots of opportunity to practice. The universe was showing me what I still needed to heal: my judgment of others, my deep sadness, my emergency bogus calls, my irritability, and my bitterness.

I got a hint of my bitterness when I was watching a wedding invitation in the form of a video on DVD rather than the usual paper invitation you get in the mail. I watched this wonderful couple embracing their love for each other, and when it was done, I said to myself, "I wonder how long that will last?" Wow! I hadn't known I was so bitter. I didn't know what I didn't know. So there I was: a mess. I had to clean up my mess. Easier said than done.

I know this works because it worked for me. It has worked for literally hundreds of clients that I have worked with over the years. So don't give up. Our humanness and our feelings are the gateways to our healing and our essence. The love of your life is you!

If you are spinning or sick and tired of being sick and tired, you may be being nudged to take a deeper look at your life and be what you are capable of being. Look at what you are here to heal, the suffering in your world.

It is common when you are spinning not to remember who you really are. You get caught up in the spinning. Are you proud of who you are, especially when no one is around?

It is important to deal with the limitations of being human, our frailties. It is much more healthy to grapple with our frailties than pretend they don't exist. This is living a more authentic life. Love is the answer to every question. Choosing who you want to be and standing for that is your true power.

For example, I used to think that once a moment had passed, you couldn't get it back. I have challenged this thought, especially in therapy. Sometimes, a thing will be said in a therapy session and I don't respond. I think that moment is lost, or later I think of a better way to handle the situation. I have learned that I can always go back and readdress or clarify. I used to often talk myself out of revisiting the situation. I have found that every time I have gone back and said what I wanted to say, it has been positive.

You can go back and capture the essence of the moment. That is the beginning of a good practice, and sometimes it means making amends. I encourage clients to go back and address the issues that are unresolved. Sometimes it can be as simple as admitting to their loved one that they were right; saying clearly, "I am here for you";

or saying, "I care enough about you to address this issue and let you know I think about you and you matter to me." Sometimes, it can be the turning point in a relationship.

What I know about the universe is that if you miss the opportunity to go back, there will always be another opportunity to heal. The circumstances may change but the content is the same. The universe will present a similar situation so you can heal. You can't do this wrong. It will keep coming up over and over again to heal, if you are willing to notice and grow. What have you noticed that has been coming over and over again? Write it down. You may even start noticing that you have handled it differently than you would have handled it in the past. Good Work. Good Practice.

CHAPTER 8

Multigenerational Patterns

If you haven't noticed yet, I find it fascinating how human beings think and especially how I think. In-to-me-see. This is what I have come here to heal. My oldest brother said to me once, "I know why you went into social work. You want to figure out why we are the way we are." I laughed at the time. A part of me knew he was right. I didn't know at the time just how right he was.

It has been my experience that we repeat our problems until they get healed. Often when you make a connection between yourself and your parents or family members it is an "a-ha" moment. For example, are you always attracted to a type of person who is not good for you? Did you swear that you wouldn't be like your parents, then find yourself doing the same thing your parents did or said?

This happens through innocence. You are born into a family, and sometimes you feel that the people in your family are hurting. You don't know how to make it better. An innocent child may try to help out, be comic relief, be seen and not heard, be really good, or do anything that stops the pain in the family. The child seeks a role that minimizes, diverts, or distracts the pain in the family.

Sometimes, if you were such a child, you learn that you don't matter or that you are not enough. Somehow you pick up or feel that you are responsible for your parents' pain.

Do you have a lot of alcoholics in your life? Is your life chaotic? Is there a lot of drama? You know that something isn't right here. Something inside of you is letting you know that you are ready to change. You would not feel it or see it if it wasn't ready to come up and heal.

How do you heal? How do you do it differently when doing the same thing feels comfortable, familiar, and safe? Don't be afraid. Trust the process. Your feelings will be your way out of pain. These situations wouldn't come into your consciousness unless they were ready to heal. It's that simple.

These problems can also be multigenerational. Are you ready to heal? If you can't heal, how do you expect others to heal? Show them the way rather than expecting them to change. You are the one you have been waiting for—no longer an innocent child, rather an adult willing to look at your feelings and do things differently.

In therapy, a client with an alcoholic parent noticed that they were constantly trying to help their parent. They came to therapy to ask, "Why do they do that? They shouldn't do that. How could they do that to our family?" The client was trying to heal the family pattern.

The client and the parent were both addicts: the parent was addicted to alcohol, and the client was addicted to helping the parent. One addiction may appear more acceptable than the other; however, both of them were suffering. We heal through relationships in our families, work, and community.

The good news is that these patterns wouldn't be showing up unless you were ready to heal. These patterns are learned behavior, and they can be unlearned. Healthy boundaries and habits can be nurtured. If you expect them to change, and if your happiness depends on someone else changing, then you will not get the result you want. It is more important for *you* to change. You do it and show them the way.

You are the only one you can change. This is good news, because your happiness doesn't depend on someone else. This is that 100 percent responsibility. It is the only way I know out of the spinning and being sick and tired of being sick and tired.

Another example of family patterns repeating themselves is that sometimes, when a child is adopted later in life, they recreate their own adoption. Only this time, they are the parent making the decision. Some make the choice to place their child for adoption, while others choose to keep their child. Fortunately, now there are many options for birth parents and adoptive parents, such as open adoption. Birth parents are also able to choose the adopting parents. It is all part of their healing. Adopted children can heal their own feelings of abandonment or unresolved questions by repeating patterns or making a different choice. It's how we heal through relationships. This often means repeating family patterns.

We may develop a different form of the same pattern. Your parents may be addicted to alcohol, while you may be addicted to work. These patterns are usually learned very young. Generally, children do what they have learned. You learn how to cope in your family.

One of my clients was yelled at when they were very young, around three years of age. They could see how this event shaped their whole life. They avoided any situation where they thought they would get yelled at, so much so that it limited their life choices and activities.

What pattern or thought is running your life? Where is it for you in your life? It may not be yelling. What are you avoiding? Once this avoidance pattern was brought to light, the client could see it coming. The client made a conscious decision to walk through the fear, real or imagined, and come out the other side victoriously.

It may sound simple and insignificant. You may be wondering how this could impact someone's life. It did. This fear of being yelled at and disappointing someone else was running my client's life. It became an obsession, and they didn't even know it.

Freedom is making choices with "you," your higher self—not your ego. Your ego will keep you small and suffering every time. Understand your ego. This is knowledge, and knowledge is power.

There may be something that you have been suffering with for a very long time. Take a look at what event or pattern you are obsessing about. Where does this fit in your life? Thoughts like "I'm different," "I don't belong," or "I'm not supposed to be here" all have the same impact. Find out what thought is running your life.

I had a client who grew up with the thought, "I don't belong here." In trying to find out when this thought began, it became apparent that it wasn't even their thought. It was their mother's thought. Their mother was German, and when she came to Canada shortly after the Second World War, she felt she didn't belong here. Her child, my client, grew up and took on this belief. My client didn't know this thought was running their life. They felt they didn't belong in their family, at school, at work, or in their community.

What beliefs are you holding on to that may not even be yours? Just look and see if there is something there for you. Ask a close friend. Sometimes things are so close, they are hard to see.

Here is another example of the message "I don't belong." A client was the youngest of seven children. She had six older brothers. When she was born, her mother said, "I don't know what to do with a girl." The story was told over and over in the family, and the little girl internalized the message. She and her ego looked for all the proof and found it. She didn't belong at home, nor at school, nor in her marriage, nor as a mother. This thought was running her life.

This message "I don't belong" became very vivid for me when I was listening to an interview with Dr. David Suzuki. He talked about his childhood, when his family was put in a Japanese Canadian internment camp during World War II. His family lost their home and all their belongings. They were uprooted from Ontario and put in a camp in Northern British Columbia. He recalled how he looked Japanese, so he didn't fit in with the white children, and he didn't speak Japanese, so he didn't fit in with the Japanese children. He was left with the message "I don't belong."

I thought if a famous, confident, successful Canadian academic, science broadcaster, and environmental activist got this message, similar to the one that so many of my clients got, then perhaps it permeates our human psyche and experience.

Where is it that you don't belong? Take a moment and look. Remember, your ego doesn't want you to find where you don't belong. Your ego is probably saying, "No, that's not your experience." Just sit with it for a few moments and look.

Where don't you belong? We keep repeating the pattern until it is healed. Just notice the patterns in your life. What messages did you grow up with that make you angry, frustrated, or sad? Messages are often multigenerational. The ones I see often in therapy are:

- People don't understand me
- People don't appreciate me
- No one loves me
- I'm unlovable
- I don't know what to do
- I can't do this
- I'm not smart enough
- I don't have enough money
- I don't matter
- I'm not worthy
- I can never get ahead

What messages did you grow up with in your family? Write them down. What messages did you inherit? What messages did your family give you over and over again? Notice. Write them down.

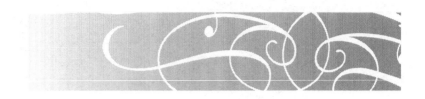

CHAPTER 9

The Form Is Different but the Content Is the Same

I have given this concept a separate chapter because once you recognize this concept, it is very helpful. Like double dipping, you'll see it everywhere. In the preceding chapter, I gave four examples of the same message: "I don't belong." They were different. One was about being conceived out of wedlock. One was about someone from a different country. One was about birth order and gender. One was about a traumatic experience. In the end, the same thought of "I don't belong" left people feeling small and suffering.

Just notice: where are you feeling small and suffering? What are you telling yourself, and what have others told you? Look particularly at your family, community, and society. Look to see where these thoughts have originated.

When I ask people when they first felt they didn't belong, they very seldom remember. If they sit with it and try to go back, though, they always find it. It's about taking the time to look and shine a light on the darkness.

I also gave the example of a client's parent who was addicted to alcohol. The client became addicted to figuring out why their parent was addicted to alcohol. That is what innocence does sometimes. This client was stuck. They become so consumed with helping that they never had to look at themselves. "Helping" can be the most effective form of deflection and denial.

Find out what you are addicted to. It may look different. It still leaves you small and suffering. The most ultimate way I know to help your loved ones is to find out what your addiction is, heal yourself first, and show them there is another way.

If you have ever been on a plane and listened to the instructions regarding a possible emergency event that results in oxygen masks dropping down, you will notice that they instruct you to put your oxygen mask on first before you attempt to help others. This is a very good metaphor for what I am talking about here. Focusing on yourself and then helping others in your life is most effective. It's okay. You are not being selfish. You are practicing good self-care.

I have worked with a lot of parents of children who are acting out. Their children are angry, violent, disrespectful, engaging in dangerous behavior, and ignoring family rules and boundaries. It has been my experience that children are the barometers of the stress, violence, and chaos in their homes. A child shows symptoms of what is happening in the home; a child is not the problem in the home.

Children are often the cause of the family seeking help. Parents become frustrated, overwhelmed, and consumed with feelings of being bad parents. Children are often saying with their behavior that something is wrong here. They act out for help.

I encourage parents to focus on themselves, not their children. It has been my experience that the better the parents do, the better their children do, and not the other way around. Children are waiting for their parents to show up for them. The best way parents can show up for their children is to heal themselves, their addictions, their destructive behavior, and the chaos in the home.

It doesn't mean things will become perfect. There will always be challenges. You will be better able to handle those challenges when you understand you. "In-to-me-see." If you can deal with your addictions and struggles, you will be showing your children how to deal with their struggles. As a parent, you are always role modeling. Even when you are asleep, you are role modeling. You are either role modeling good sleep habits or unhealthy sleep habits. You get to choose. You set the standard in your home.

This is not a good time for "do what I say, not what I do." Children will find the discrepancies and call you on them every time. If it isn't safe to tell you verbally, they will tell you with their actions. Are you listening?

What are the discrepancies in your home? Write them down. What do you tell your children to do that you are not doing? Write it down. What unresolved issues are you not willing to look at? Your children will let you know something is wrong if you are listening. If you don't listen, things tend to escalate. Are things escalating? Write down your concerns.

In the previous two chapters, I talked about family patterns, being human, and being stuck in negative patterns of mad and sad. You will read often in this book that the form is different but the content is the same. Mad and sad have many forms: anger, depression, procrastination, boredom, and addictions. You may find that you know a lot of the information in this book. However, knowing something on an intellectual basis is different from knowing it on a cellular level. I know a lot of bookaholics; I'm one of them. Because you have read about something does not mean you have incorporated it into your life.

It's time to put information into action. You can't think your way out of your suffering; you have to act your way out by doing things differently. Actions speak louder than words. For example, I knew about projection long before I studied it. Projection is the unconscious transfer of one's own desire or emotions to another person. It is when you feel, think, or see something, and then articulate that another person is feeling, thinking, or seeing that thing. I feel sad; therefore everyone is sad. When you see how projection is alive in your life, playing out in every relationship at home, at work, and in your community, your awareness is heightened. I hope your awareness becomes very heightened. Let it touch you on a cellular level.

Going back to the examples of clients who felt they did not belong, this feeling started off as a learned message that crept into every aspect of their lives. When they went to elementary school, they were teased by classmates and felt they didn't belong. In high school, they were bullied and felt they didn't belong. In their marriages, they were abused and felt they didn't belong. In every job they had, they felt they didn't belong.

This may appear overly simplistic. Nevertheless, understanding and knowledge will only get you so far. I encourage you to look, experience, feel, and act. Walk through those thoughts, challenge them, acknowledge your humanness, and expose the thoughts for what they are—fear. Fear can be read as an acronym: *f*alse *e*vidence *a*ppearing *r*eal.[4] It can also be read as *f*eeling *e*xcited and *r*eady.[5] You get to choose.

Wherever you are in your journey to find out what you are here to heal, look for the patterns that are being played over and over again. You are able to change the world—your world. Your world is the only world you can change. When you change your world, the world changes.

CHAPTER 10

Old Paradigm: War—Divide and Conquer

The strategy of "divide and conquer" is a very old strategy that has been in practice since the beginning of time. It is war. When you choose divide and conquer, you choose war. When you choose love, you choose peace.

What better way to split humanity than to pit good against bad, men against women, blacks against whites, east against west, north against south, Christians against Muslims, city against country, unskilled against skilled, employee against employer, or educated against uneducated? The ego likes complexity and confusion. War serves to detach, isolate, and estrange people, leading to rejection and feelings of being disenfranchised. Just notice when you are choosing war over peace in your life, family, community, and country.

Historically, we have been taught to distrust strangers. Hundreds of years ago, strangers often unknowingly brought and spread diseases from city to city and country to country. More recently, we follow cases of swine or bird flu, Ebola virus, and Zika. This fear of strangers has its roots in very practical and legitimate concerns.

However, it spreads like wildfire through the fabric of the human psyche. Fear of the unknown can be used as a blanket to blind and spread confusion. Did you catch the ego traps in that sentence? There are at least two: *trying to understand* and *confusion*. Remember: if you are confused, your ego is running your life.

It usually only takes a few seconds for you to decide whether you like someone or not. Add a little fear, skepticism, anxiety, or insecurity, and you have war.

Historically speaking, women were the property of men, whether their fathers or their husbands. Women couldn't own property because they were property. They couldn't get an education, work outside the home, or vote.

I believe men and women were meant to complement one another. I often use the analogy of flight and the wings of a bird. If both wings are strong and respected, then the bird can fly. If one wing is too strong or too weak, then the bird flies in circles. Women and men fly strongly when both are respected for their differences and honored for what they bring to a discussion.

This is not about winning or comparing; it is about how you play. There is no winner or loser. We all lose when one group is denied equality with another group. It is often said that in the body, the masculine part is the hard skeleton and the feminine part is the softer muscles around the skeleton. Both are needed to survive and move with grace.

The yin in Chinese philosophy is the passive female principle of the universe, characterized as earth and dark. This is in contrast with yang, the active male principle of the universe, characterized as heat and light. Yin and yang are meant to be in contrast, both interconnected and interdependent. Both are needed to create life. When these two forces are in harmony, life flourishes.

If we were all the same, it would be very boring. Diversity is like a flower garden. Can you say that a daffodil is more beautiful than an azalea? Different flowers in our garden give contrast, texture, shape, color, depth, and richness to our lives, as do different languages, cultures, and sizes of people.

I have worked in the field of domestic violence for many years. Generally speaking, men feel that women are against them, and women feel that men are against them. There you have it: two camps pitted against each other. It's good old divide and conquer. Once you start working with this concept, you will see it everywhere.

Needless to say, nothing will ever get resolved from this kind of limited thinking. Questioning it is a start and a good start. It gets the dialogue going. However, the conversation needs to go deeper. Just notice. Where does divide and conquer play out in your life? Who are you at war with? What or whom are you trying to control or change?

The even deeper question is, "Can you change you?" You expect others to change. Can you change?

In my experience, whenever you have the haves and the have-nots, the powerful and the powerless, then the haves and the powerful generally do not share well. They perceive it as not in their best interest to share.

Slavery demonstrates the principle of divide and conquer at work. A colonial economy is based on using cheap labor and slave labor. Sound familiar? Things have not changed that much. Why are large multinationals going to other markets? Our multinational companies are our plantation slave owners. Cheaper labor gives bigger profits. Slavery is not dead; we have just shifted it a bit out of sight.

Another example of divide and conquer is our penitentiary system. It is disproportionately filled with the poor, the disenfranchised, and minorities. It is our history, it doesn't have to be our future.

I have had the pleasure of working with men and women, rich and poor, black and white, immigrants and indigenous people. In North America, one in four women have been sexually abused and one in six men have been sexually abused. This is not a gendered issue, even though it may be presented that way. Sexual abuse is a gross misuse of power, regardless of gender. Gender is used to confuse the issue. Gender is a misnomer or a red herring. Divide and conquer is at work rather than addressing the deeper issue. Make anything a gender issue and you have war. Just notice. Have you had enough war yet? When what you are doing doesn't work for you anymore, just notice. War does not get you the results you want.

Another misconception is that domestic violence is a men-against-women issue, women-against-men or a gender issue. Domestic violence is actually a society problem. This is another example of divide and conquer at work. Gender gets used to divide people, and the injustice goes unresolved. It took men and women to put life on the moon. It will take women and men to end domestic violence, slavery, poverty, belief in scarcity, suffering, and all war, starting with the war within ourselves that we project onto others.

Before I end this chapter, I would like to address language and the use of language to control, anger, and dominate. We give everything its meaning. We collectively determine what is good, bad, helpful, valuable, useful, or significant. We have developed symbols called *letters* so we can understand and explain things to each other. We have all agreed that you are reading a book. We call it a book so we all know what we are speaking about. When we read the word *book*, we all have a shared idea of what we are talking about. We give labels to things to differentiate them from other things. The power of words and their meaning is paramount in communication.

There is a particular word I have grown to love, though most people abhor it. I love educating people about its original meaning. People shrink, recoil, and even shudder at it.

I was working with women in a female court-mandated group, meaning all the participants were women who were legally charged, convicted of assault, and sentenced to attend a sixteen-week program. Well, needless to say, they were not generally enthusiastic about attending group.

During a session, we were talking about triggers of our anger. We came up with names that people call women: *bitch, whore, slut.* The worst thing to be called was *cunt.* My intention was to find out what these words actually meant, in the hope of taking out the sting and minimizing the trigger.

So I went on my computer and searched for the meanings of these words. *Bitch* is the correct term for a female dog. *Whore* means unclean. *Slut* means low standards of cleanliness.

Then there was the dreaded *C* word, *cunt.* Before *cunt* became a derogatory term, it was a poetic term meaning "flower of the flesh" or "cave of love." You will find the definition in the *Old Oxford English Dictionary.* It is always good to check things out for yourself. Ask and become tenacious for the truth.

What the word *cunt* has taught me is that we give everything its meaning. We, as a society, collectively decide if a word is beautiful or ugly, a compliment or an insult. Trust me, when someone calls me a cunt, I say thank you. Knowledge takes all the power and sting out of the word. We give every word its power or not. I encourage you to choose whatever meaning is most loving to you!

Unfortunately, words can be meant to be hurtful. It doesn't mean we have to take them that way. We always have a choice. This is where your power lies—in the choosing. Make a loving choice to you. Don't take anything personally.

When I talk about this in group, I usually get the response "It's easy for you say" or "How can you not take it personally?" It depends—do you still want war in your life? You get to decide. Are you sick and tired of being sick and tired with the war in your life? An insult says more about the person trying to insult you than it does about you. Can you slow down the spinning enough to see that this is possible? Can you be with it and let them have their opinion? That is all it is, an opinion. You just haven't looked at it that way before.

I encourage you to look at things differently, especially if they anger, upset, or sadden you. Write down what your trigger words are and what people say that pushes your buttons. Can you slow down the spinning enough to make a conscious choice rather than give a knee-jerk reaction?

If you choose war, you may get some immediate relief. Unfortunately, this will not give you what you want—peace. We want unconditional love. Can we give it? If we can't give it, it can't be done. "No, they should give it first, and then I will give it." Sound familiar? Did you catch the *should*? "I will love you when you do what I want" or "I will support you when you do what I want." This is all conditional.

War is very seductive. When you start working with these concepts, you begin to take back your mind. Slow down the spinning to stay present and choose the future you want to live into. That is true power. A mature mind doesn't do war. There is nothing in war except suffering and sadness.

There is another framework I share that people find very helpful in discerning the spinning and war in their lives. It is commonly called "the drama triangle" and was coined by psychotherapist Stephen Karpman.[6] It is an ineffective response to conflict in a social model of human interaction. In simple terms, when you are struggling in unhealthy relationships, you tend to take on the role of rescuer, victim, or perpetrator. Learning to identify these roles, and then practicing recognizing when you are being the rescuer, victim, or perpetrator is a powerful way to heighten your awareness and catch the spinning in your life.

When we are in the old paradigm of war, we fluctuate between roles. Sometimes we can fluctuate between them within minutes, in the course of a single conversation. For example, we often get into relationships to "help" another. There are four kinds of rescue. First, you are rescuing when you do something for someone that they could do for themselves. Second, you are rescuing if you do something for someone that they haven't asked you to do. Third, you are recuing if you are putting more energy into someone else's problem than they are. Last, you know you have been rescuing when you realize that you don't really want to do what you are doing for another person, and you come to resent them. Another way of saying this is you can't say no without feeling guilty, and so you consistently put other people's needs before your own.

If any of these situations describes you, write down the situation and with whom you feel this way.

Here is an example: a *marshmallow parent* has few rules or boundaries. They are often very loving and warm. They are too busy or too insecure to enforce limits with their children. They do everything for their children, and the children are ungrateful, take advantage, or don't return the help. The parent ends up feeling used.

The marshmallow parent is a good example of a rescuer. Some people feel guilty if they don't rescue. They can't stop rescuing even when it is not in their best interest or may even hurt them. If this describes you, write down the situation and with whom you feel this way.

Eventually the rescuer shifts to the victim. The very person or institution you have tried to rescue turns on you, doesn't appreciate you, or says something hurtful to you. You feel victimized. If you feel this way, write down the situation and with whom you feel this way.

In abusive relationships, this escalates. When you are feeling bullied, threatened, disrespected, or mistreated, you feel like a victim. This can only go on for so long until you get angry, fight back, or defend yourself. Then you become the persecutor.

All three of the positions in the drama triangle are suffering. Where are you suffering? What is your favorite place to be in the triangle? Notice if you flip back and forth. If you are honest, you probably have been all three. Sometimes you can be all three in thirty seconds or less. Just notice and write it down.

Often when people become the persecutor, they seek help, especially if they are conscious enough to know this is not who they want to be. They realize the situation has gotten totally out of control and what they are doing is not helping.

Defending oneself can be especially unhelpful. Defense is the first act of war. Catch yourself when you feel the need to defend yourself, because you are on your way to suffering.

There are other people for whom the persecutor role is their go-to position. They have found that this usually gets them what they want. They can bully, throw a temper tantrum, intimidate, and use their position or power inappropriately. The confusing part is they are not persecutors all the time. They are very loving and supportive sometimes, often most of the time.

Did you catch the word *confusing*? The ego loves confusion.

I'm not saying you don't get to protest and share your truth. You are not a doormat. You have the right to your opinion. It is important to have a voice. What I am suggesting is a complete paradigm shift, and that is the shift to love.

So what would that shift look like? When I ask people, they are usually at a loss. What I propose is caring, not rescuing. Caring is when you want to help others, not when you feel responsible for others. This is where discernment comes in.

Caring and rescuing sound so close—how do you discern? The only way I know is to heighten your awareness. Notice when you feel responsible for something that you didn't do. This can get very tricky, because your ego may tell you, for example, that your child's problem is yours. Your ego may be right, even so it may not be telling you this for the right reason.

The good news is that behavior is learned and therefore, can be unlearned. Healthier behaviors can be learned and replace old patterns.

The other way to discern whether you are caring or rescuing is to notice when you start to suffer and become sad. This is why it is so important to listen to your feelings. If you are suffering, you are often rescuing.

When I am rescuing, I am fixing. When I am caring, I am listening and supportive. When I am rescuing, I feel tired, anxious and responsible. When I am caring, I feel relaxed and aware. When I am rescuing, I am concerned with solutions, answers and being right. When I am caring, I am concerned with being present, feelings, and the other person.

When I am caring. I expect the other person to be responsible for themselves and their own actions. Letting go doesn't mean you don't care. It means you can't do it for someone else. Can you do it for you?

CHAPTER 11

New Paradigm: Love—Inclusion and Acceptance

Remember the introduction, when I shared that the answer to every question is love? Well, it is time to revisit that statement. It can be tricky to discern what love is and what love isn't, especially when you are listening to your ego and you don't realize it. By now you have heightened your awareness enough to recognize when you are listening to your ego and when you are listening to "you," your higher self. You know that there is another way.

Very simply, ask you. When you listen to your ego, you will feel upset, confused, discontented, uncertain, ambivalent, or bored. You may doubt yourself. When you listen to "you," you will feel clarity, lightness, peace, and serenity.

Practice noticing. It's about not giving in and not giving up. It's about standing clear in your truth. It's saying what is so for you and asking for what you need.

Slow down the spinning enough to ask you. You are the seed from which many things can grow. You have everything you need in this moment. It is time to ask you what you feel, think, and genuinely want to do. There is a coming together based on love, compassion for others, and particularly compassion for yourself. You are healing.

It can feel very subtle at first. With practice it will feel clearer and stronger.

Don't be surprised if your ego goes into overdrive with this practice. Your ego will tell you that you are crazy. More subtly, your ego may tell you that I am crazy, a quack. What is your ego telling you? Practice being the listener and know that those thoughts are not you. You are the listener, and you get to choose what thoughts to believe and act upon. This is where your true power lies—in choosing who you want to be. Test them out for yourself.

Remember: your ego doesn't want you to get this. It thinks it is going to die. What would you do if you thought you were going to die? You would try every means to stay alive and stop you from getting this. Your ego wants to live and be in charge. How else do you think we have been so unconscious for so long?

So what is love? Your ego will tell you lots of things. Listen to what it is saying. Write those things down in your journal. If you think love is attraction, lust, pleasure, and sex, then your ego is giving you a very shallow view of love.

Generally speaking, the ego is right. Human beings don't love; they want something. We want to feel valued, loved, whole, complete, understood, cherished, safe, and even powerful. We will do pretty much anything to achieve those feelings. Just notice. Write down what comes to mind.

There is so much more to love. Your purpose is to see the world through love, with true vision and divinity. When you truly love, there is no sacrifice, no agenda. It just is or it isn't. You get to ask for what you need and even protest.

I'm not asking you to be a doormat. That is the ego's view of love. It is just done differently, from a place of compassion and truth, not from fear, obligation, and guilt. It is very simple. Just try it. This is what taking 100 percent responsibility for your life looks like. It will feel funny and even uncomfortable in the beginning, especially when you start by loving yourself first. Everything you want from your partner, your parents, your children, your job, or your community—you give it to you.

It only matters that you understand you, that you value you, that you complete you, that you be the love of your life. You cannot make another person love you. Can you love you? That is the task at hand. That is the real question. That is the deeper conversation. If you love you, it doesn't matter if they love you. Your happiness doesn't depend on anyone else's approval.

I can hear the ego saying, "How selfish. What is she saying? Love myself? Of course I love myself." What is your ego saying? Just notice and write it down.

Every person is required to grapple with their humanness, with all its bumps, bruises, and frailties, and rise to the love and divinity in all of us. That is the essence of our journey here on this earth.

Who is going to run the car of your life, your ego or your soul? Are you sick and tired of being sick and tired yet? Your ego will tell you that you have to fight for what you want, that it's too hard, that you've wasted your money buying this book, and that I'm crazy. Listen and write down what your ego is saying to you. If you are sick and tired of being sick and tired, ask yourself: is war working for you and getting you what you want?

What I am proposing is the opposite of war. Love is not really new. This new paradigm has been around for a very long time. There has been so much confusion and misunderstanding about love that it has made love almost ridiculous.

The ego has been spinning long enough. It is time for clarity. When someone asks me, "Who are you?" I answer, "I am love incarnate." You and I are love in human form. You haven't seen yourself that way before, so it may feel very uncomfortable. You might think I've lost it. Or you might say that's what I want to be. That's what I try to be. Somehow, it just doesn't work out that way.

We are love incarnate. Love is in us. We are love, and our essence is love. When you love from this place, you want for people what they want. You get to decide if you can offer it—not from a place of lack, insecurity, guilt, or manipulation, rather from a place of "It's okay to say no." Sometimes saying no is saying yes to yourself. It's not giving in or giving up. It's standing in your truth.

This is what I call a deeper conversation. It only takes one to change. It's easy to love those who love you back or do what you want. This is about loving yourself enough to love it all: the good, the bad, and the ugly. Love unconditionally.

I'm not saying the past is right. I'm saying it doesn't get to define you now. Our history does not get to define us. We cannot change the past. We can stay present enough to give ourselves a different future.

Remember, you are loved much more than you know. Everything has got you to where you are right now. It is important to not judge your journey. There is no other place to be than right here. You are in the perfect place for you. Have you noticed that wanting something different only robs you of the joy that is possible right now?

So what do you do now? Is your ego having a heyday yet? Write down what your ego is telling you. Do you believe your ego? Or are you slowing down the spinning enough to be the observer, the listener who gets to choose what you believe? This is where your true power lies, in the choosing.

I'll say it again. So what do you do now? What does love look like in your life from now on? There is no magic pill to swallow; there is only practice. Your ego has not given up on controlling you and never will, just so you know. However, you can deal with your ego differently. You are liberating yourself and your ego at the same time through unconditional love. You are understanding your true self and integrating it with your ego. You are loving all of you, even the parts that are unflattering, addicted, obsessed, confused, scared, irrational, and unloving.

Life will always have challenges. I still get caught. I call it "jumping in and out of the nightmare." This is not about doing it perfectly. I notice and hopefully I jump out really quickly. Then I laugh. In that moment I get to choose fear, my past or who I want to be in that moment. I can choose the highest expression of myself. I talk to my ego, and we have a great life together. It's about loving every part of you and loving your ego.

The ego has not died as it feared. It is still so easy for us to fall back into old habits. The ego has been watching over, protecting, and explaining to keep you safe. It has done its job. You are still alive. This is about doing things differently. Liberate yourself and your ego into the love that you are and is your birthright. This is what you have come here to do: heal yourself into your highest integrated self, which is love. The ego and you together as love—this is your true essence.

It looks different for different people. This is not about comparing yourself to others or being something you are not for others. Did you catch the ego traps of *comparing* and *unrealistic expectations*? Keep your practice alive.

What I know about human beings is that we want to contribute, connect, and share. A client wished that everyone could be in a group with me and asked me to write a book. That is what human beings do—they find something that works for them, and they want to share it with those they love. I alleviate the pain in my world first, and then I share what I have learned with others. I am always practicing. Challenges will continue to present themselves, and then I have another opportunity to do it differently.

It's important to ask yourself if you want the suffering to stop. When you stop the suffering in your life, the world will change. That has been my experience. Give it a try. You have nothing to lose except your suffering.

Notice whether you really want the suffering to stop. Sometimes people's identities become the suffering. Suffering makes them feel alive. It makes them feel real. Who would you be without your suffering?

I can't change you. However, I can change me. Once I change, the world changes. I don't know exactly how it changes. You have that power and effect.

A client shared that she thought she had lost her eldest child. She felt she had neglected him. It was easier not to confront him and just take care of the younger children. I said I thought that he was waiting for her to be the parent and show him the way. She risked and spoke to her eldest child. That family has a new relationship today, built on that one conversation that led to many different conversations. This client changed her world by not selling out on herself. Instead, she became the parent her child needed and she wanted to be. There is a closeness between them now that was unimaginable before they stood in their truth, a treasured and a sacred relationship. When you change, the world changes.

How to change starts with you. Once I surrendered my spinning and stopped trying to change the situation, I have not looked back. If you can change, there is hope for everyone else. However, if your happiness depends on them changing, then you will be waiting for a very long time. Don't wait. Show them the way. Give yourself what you need to be happy. It may be trust, appreciation, gratitude, or peace. Just notice and be the love of your life.

I bought a T-shirt for one of my sons. It was printed with the Zen proverb, "The obstacle is the path." We both loved the T-shirt for many reasons. I loved that he wore it. I loved the message. He loved to wear it because he thought the saying was interesting, the T-shirt fit him well, and it was a great conversation starter. It is important to find the divine in all things, even the obstacles. It is not the situation that is the problem—it is your thoughts about the situation, or what you make it mean. Love finds the grace, strength, and courage. Through awareness and conscious living, you can live a new paradigm.

I've seen other proverbs. "There is no way to peace. Peace is the way." "There is no path to happiness. Happiness is the path." These have been popularized. In other words, be happy now. You don't have to wait for it or pursue it. Be it. Be happiness. Skip the future and be happy now. This is a state of being, not doing. There is nothing to do. It is about who you are.

If I were going to hide love, I would hide love in each and every one of us. Love is so close. Our love is that close. We are all one. Find the divine in all things.

What a treasure is to be found in each and every one of us. See someone without judgment about their skin color, religion, sex, or past deeds. I see compassion. What do you see? Write it down.

If what you are doing isn't loving, then ask yourself why it isn't. There is usually a reason, whether it makes sense or not. What is important is for you to look at it with new eyes.

A very dear friend taught me that all behavior is purposeful.[7] One aspect of choice theory, developed by psychiatrist William Glasser, states that all behavior is purposeful and motivated to satisfy our five basic needs: to love and belong, to be powerful, to be free, to have fun, and to survive.

Look at your behavior. What behaviors do you do to be loved, give you a sense of belonging, make you feel powerful, be autonomous, create fun, and survive? What behaviors and thoughts are running your life?

There is often a gift in every situation if we are willing to look. What is your ego telling you now? Write it down.

I didn't want my mother to die. Unfortunately, she did, and there was nothing I could do about it. I had to let go. All I could do was be grateful for the time I had with her and learn from her life.

There are many ways to sabotage your own life. Are you robbing yourself? There are many ways to rob your life. Perhaps you are robbing your children of a parent who is present and conscious? Be still a moment and see if there is anything robbing you of your life.

Dr. Tony White wrote a book called *Working with Suicidal Individuals* (2011).[8] It is very helpful in identifying seven suicide decisions. These decisions are made early in life. If certain circumstances (usually loss or trauma) are present, then suicide may be chosen as a solution to suffering and pain in a person's life.

My experience in domestic violence has given me a heightened awareness of suicide conversations. You can identify suicidal decisions, such as "If you don't change, I will kill myself."

"If things get too bad, I will kill myself."

"I will show you even if it kills me."

"I will get you to kill me."

"I will kill myself by accident."

"I will kill myself to hurt you."

"I will almost die (over and over) to get you to love me."

Many people who are suicidal during group feel they shouldn't be in group therapy because they are taking a space that someone else could use. They feel unworthy of being present. They feel the group would be better off without them, their partner would be better off without them, and their children would be better off without them. They feel they are a burden to themselves and everyone in their lives.

Some people think that suicidal individuals are selfish. Such individuals are actually in a very dark place, where they don't matter and can't see that ever changing. During group, I stress the value suicidal individuals bring to group just by opening the conversation about suicide. They provide the space for a deeper conversation.

Usually, when I ask around the room, everyone has had thoughts of suicide at some time in their lives. It is important to look at the trauma and challenges in your life differently. I'm not saying what has happened to you is right. I'm just saying that I can't change it and you can't change it. Possibly, what has happened can be a catalyst for change. Looking at it differently may be helpful.

Where are these conversations in your life? Where are you killing yourself over and over again? Are you taking pills, drinking alcohol, doing risky behavior? Are you in constant chaos and drama? Are you living in unsafe conditions? Are you suffering every day?

During group, people often cry. I encourage them to cry—to let go and let their tears wash their hearts. When you have an open mind, it opens the heart. They have held in those tears for so long, some people are afraid they will never stop crying. Eventually, they do. Often people have accumulated several traumas. It is important to cry for all of the traumatic events that you have not allowed yourself to acknowledge. Grieve that they happened to you. Trust the process. Let love and the tears wash your heart. Feel everything. Your feelings are your way out. You will stop crying when you have grieved it all. You will be okay. Actually, you will be better than okay. You will heal. Do not deny yourself any healing or your true nature of love.

After being on this path of healing for a while, it is hard to watch the people in your life suffer with their thoughts. It is natural to want to help. However, it is important to remember when you were unaware and had those thoughts too. It is important not to feel superior. Have compassion for them. You were not ready until you were ready. They are just like you.

In the meantime, until they are ready, show them the way by your actions. The way out of the suffering, particularly the negative thoughts, is doing things differently. Support them and guide them. It is important for them to know that they can walk through the pain and come out the other side, peacefully and full of love, rather than with disappointment, shame, disgust, and fearfulness.

When talking about self-actualization, it is hard not to use Maslow's hierarchy of needs to explain human motivation.[9] I have mentioned it because I would like to propose a twist. You may be familiar with the triangle that denotes the process of motivation, from food and shelter at the bottom to self-actualization at the tip of the triangle. I propose that the triangle be inverted. I propose that there is room for everyone at the top. To become self-actualized is not just for a select few at the top of the pyramid, as its shape implies. Rather, there is room for everyone at the top.

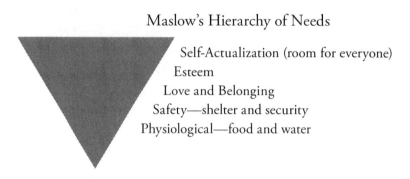

Maslow's Hierarchy of Needs

Self-Actualization (room for everyone)
Esteem
Love and Belonging
Safety—shelter and security
Physiological—food and water

Everyone I have worked with is striving for a better way. It is part of the human condition.

If you are honest with yourself, you will be a little frightened about this, because we are addicted to our separateness. What will separate us from them, the haves from the have-nots, the special from the not-special, the enlightened from the unenlightened, the successful from the unsuccessful? How do we separate ourselves, stand out, and not lose ourselves?

What is your ego telling you right now? Write it down.

You may have to admit you were wrong. You may have to stretch yourself out of your comfort zone. You may find out that what you are afraid of will be what sets you free. Reality is much kinder than what we make up in our heads. When you can be with all of it—your body, mind, and soul—how exciting! You could be an example of a different way for others to be happy.

Keep noticing. When you can be with criticism, your own and others', then you know you are making progress. Growth can be challenging. Living your life from this place is yet unfamiliar. Empowerment, surrender, and 100 percent responsibility for your choices constitute a very different way to live your life. This is a new area of your birthright: love, peace, trust, wonder, faith, support, balance, patience, tolerance, compassion, and forgiveness.

There is no place to be except right where you are. Can you be happy in this moment? Just notice. Write down what you are thinking.

Do you want to be right or do you want to be happy? Open your mind enough to notice what your ego and your highest self are telling you. This is self-love. Let yourself feel. Feelings are your gateway out of suffering. Who would have guessed? Embrace your feelings. Don't deny yourself your freedom.

CHAPTER 12

Connectedness/Soul

So how do we live this new paradigm? It starts with recognizing our connectedness. I like the analogy of ice cubes. We seem separate from others, even though we really are not. That's the grand illusion. Everything is emanating from one source. We are like ice cubes. We look separate. If you heat the ice cubes, they melt into one indistinguishable puddle. Keep heating them, and they become steam and disappear. They are hydrogen and oxygen molecules, no matter what form they are in. Like those molecules, we are all connected, even though we appear separate and different.

In North American culture, we have been taught that the soul is some little thing inside of us, and when we die, it floats out of our lifeless body. Having learned and done energy work, I found it apparent that the soul is not in the body. Rather, the body is in the soul. Our souls and energy extend much farther than the confines of our bodies.

In discovering energy work, I have explored parts of myself that I didn't know existed until I looked with awe and beauty rather than fear. When I first started to learn cranial sacral therapy, I second-guessed myself and doubted what I was feeling. I would joke with my friends that a hundred years ago, they would have burned me at the stake for being a witch. I have come to honor and embrace the unknown, the unseen, and my soul, which extends much farther than my body.

There are no secrets in the soul. All is illuminated, even our deepest human frailties. The soul embraces body and mind. There is nothing to fear. Look what you have already gone through. You are still here, even if a little shaken.

There is nothing in our world we can't work through as individuals, couples, families, organizations, companies, communities, cities, provinces, states, districts, countries, and nations. We have the resources, we have the intelligence, we have capacity, and we have you. It starts with you. You have got this. We have got this, together. We are here to heal our world, together. We communicate and heal through relationships.

If your ego is saying, "Sure," or "Easy for her to say," don't listen to your ego. This is about listening to you. What do you want?

Everything has prepared you for this moment. How better to really help people than to show them the way out of suffering? Believe in them. Believe that they have everything they need to solve their own problems. There is that 100 percent responsibility thing again.

So what happens when you get stuck or blocked from resolving conflict? You keep asking for help. If I am lonely and ask a friend out, they may be busy. Then I ask another friend and another friend. Be tenacious. Use your discernment. It is much simpler than we think. Action is going to get you unstuck, not just thinking about it. Did you catch the ego trap of *trying to understand*? Keep noticing the ego traps and what is stopping you. Write it down.

Trust life that there is something bigger going on here than getting the girl/the guy, getting the car, getting the house, and who has the most stuff wins. That bigger thing is what connects us all. Choose life. Choose trust, wonder, surprise, joy, and connectedness. I invite you to explore that side of you that you can't see—the side that believes there is a better way than fear, attack, and suffering.

The ego is very seductive. It plays on all our insecurities: I don't matter, I'm not supposed to be here, no one appreciates me, I'm not enough, I'm different, they are different, I'm not smart enough, I can't do it. Can you feel the fear mounting just from reading these words? These are all different forms of the same thing: fear.

Don't believe your ego. Liberate your ego and thank your ego for bringing you this far. Thank drugs, alcohol, or your other addictions for holding you until you could see another way. It is time to keep growing, expanding, and trusting in your love and your life. You were always enough and will always be enough.

Sit with it. Don't run away from the pain you feel. Bring your pain to the surface and see it for what it is—fear. You can't solve a problem if you don't know what the problem is. Just because you can't see that you are enough or feel that you are enough doesn't mean that you are not enough. It's actually inside of you and inside of everyone.

I often ask myself, "If I were not afraid, what would I do?" Another way to say this is "If I was enough, what would I do?" That's when I know what I have to do.

We are all enough. We have all come to heal the suffering in our world. Healing the suffering in your world starts with you. You don't have to do this alone. We have all come here to heal and be our true essence, no matter what it is we are experiencing.

CHAPTER 13

Sleep, Nutrition, Exercise, Nature, Meditation, Connectedness

How do we live this new paradigm? It is important to be much kinder to yourself. We have become disconnected from our bodies. We don't feel or use our senses as they were designed. It is important to show more compassion toward ourselves. Look at the old patterns and let new, gentle ones caress you like the touch of a butterfly's wings. Slow the spinning in your mind and heighten your awareness of what is running your life.

It is important not to tighten the strings of your instrument such that the strings break. You will not be able to play the music of your life. Your enjoyment will be empty and forced. It is important to take care of your instrument. There are SIX strings I cannot stress enough in caring for the instrument of your life: sleep, nutrition, exercise, nature, meditation/relaxation, and connectedness.

First, I recommend you get enough sleep. While spinning, it is difficult to sleep. You don't want to stop because you are afraid to stop. This is often an addiction to chaos. Sometimes the chaos makes you feel alive. You fear that if you don't have chaos, you won't matter or you won't exist. Look at the chaos in your life, particularly the chaos you create yourself. You matter, whether you are spinning or not. Just notice.

Often people who have trouble sleeping develop what may appear to be odd habits. There are many things that we do naturally that may appear odd. After a loved one dies, it's quite common for the griever to sleep on the couch. The back of the couch makes the griever feel supported. You are not weird if you do that.

There are three major kinds of not sleeping: you can't fall asleep, you can't stay asleep, or you are waking every hour. You may have all three sometimes. If you can't sleep, it is usually because you are still spinning. I recommend you write down the thoughts in your head that are keeping you awake. Honor them by writing them down. Completely exhaust your mind of every thought by writing them down on paper. You will often be surprised by what happens. People tell me they've ended up writing a letter, making a list of things to do, or composing poetry when they have never written poetry before in their lives. I always keep a pen and paper by my bedside. Somehow, putting it down on paper and looking at it gets it out of your head. You can see what it is your ego is telling you.

After a traumatic experience, it is very normal not to sleep. This is a part of grieving. You are normal. Sometimes people get stuck. Family and friends may think it is time to move on. They are entitled to their opinion. You will know when it is time. Trust yourself. You'll know when you've been stuck too long for you. When my mother died, it took a year for my brain fog to lift. I actually felt it lift from my body. I didn't even know I was in a fog until it lifted. I kept going to work, and everything was back to normal—or so I had thought.

Friends and family want you to stop hurting. You have to feel the loss and then heal according to your timing, not theirs. Trust that you will know when it is time to move on and when to get help if you are stuck.

You may want to get some help from your medical doctor. You may not like taking pills, however you may want to consider it for a short period of time. Or you may try a naturopath, acupuncturist, or chiropractor for some relief. If one doesn't work, then try someone or something else. It's time to be a detective, finding what gives you relief and what works for you.

You may want to try body work: cranial sacral therapy, Reiki, massage, aromatherapy, and reflexology. I personally love yoga. I find the benefits are amazing. Not only are you moving, you are truly breathing. I find that people who experience trauma tend to hold their breath and forget to breathe. When they are breathing, it is very shallow. When you are shallow breathing, you are not getting the maximum level of oxygen to your brain and body necessary for optimum health.

Some people sleep too much. It always fascinates me that the opposite of insomnia can also be so problematic. Not enough sleep or too much sleep are both problems. It is about balance.

It is important to be tenacious about finding out what can help you get between seven and nine hours of sleep. Some people who are sleeping too much have low iron or are depressed. It's important to keep an open mind and look at all plausible causes. I have always found it easier to go to bed earlier and get up earlier than go to bed later and get up later. Technology can also influence your sleep. If possible, don't take your computer, phone, or other device into the room where you sleep. Turn off all your technology.

It is important to find out what works for you. Be tenacious for your own good health.

Second, I recommend good nutrition. I can't say enough about nutrition. It is important to slow down the spinning enough to make better choices. When you are putting healthy food into your body, it is good for both the body and the mind.

I have coached many sports and some elite athletes. I have studied recovery from sports related injuries. Over and over again, I have seen that enough sleep and a healthy diet are the two greatest factors in recovery. This goes for emotional and physical trauma recovery as well.

Sleep and nutrition are the building blocks for a different life that you are living into. It is too easy to gain time by sleeping less or skipping a meal. You are worth the extra time. It will hold you in good stead.

To achieve good nutrition, you don't have to make drastic changes. Start out small and make a few simple changes. They can make a big difference. I try to purchase organic vegetables or antibiotic-free meat when I can. I make popcorn with coconut oil and less salt.

I suggest starting out by making one recipe a week that is healthier, even if it is only a smoothie for breakfast. It can make a big difference in your overall health. It is important not to overwhelm yourself. Another easy way to improve your nutrition is to eat less processed foods. Processed food is, generally speaking, anything from a box or jar. People don't cook and prepare their own food as much as they used to. They more frequently eat out or get pre-fab food. Making this shift to eating better requires some more effort in food preparation. The benefits are worth it: a healthier you, inside, outside, and all over.

Stress can cause many side effects. I call these side effects "stress coming out sideways." You often don't get the connection. For example, I was having some bloating that became constant, and I couldn't figure it out. My abdomen was distended and became very uncomfortable. When I couldn't tighten my stomach muscles, I knew something else had to be going on.

I underwent tests and found out that I was sensitive to dairy products, such as milk, cheese, and yogurt. I was also sensitive to coffee, sesame seeds (tahini), sugar, and blueberries. A few years later, when my stress had been reduced, my sensitivities likewise became less.

Other ailments associated with stress are chronic fatigue syndrome, adrenal fatigue, fibromyalgia, colitis, and irritable bowel. As we get older, joint inflammation and constipation are common. You may want to have a full checkup.

Become persistent in taking care of your health and nutrition. Your body sends messages to you if you are listening.

Third, I recommend that you exercise.

Exercise can help you sleep better. Getting physically exhausted through exercise can help you fall asleep and get you on a regular routine of sleep. Also, exercise is the best thing to ward off diabetes, heart disease, and obesity.

Human beings are designed for movement. If you can walk, you can exercise—walking is your exercise. And there are many other options: riding a bike, hiking, swimming, roller blading, skiing, snowboarding and bowling, to name only a few. You may say you don't have time. You are worth the time. Your health depends on it.

One of my favorite routines is a small trampoline. When I watch TV, I walk on the trampoline. It is very good and doesn't cost too much. I encourage you to make small changes and build your strength in the daily practice of exercise.

People can unknowingly grow to love their chains. They cling to the old patterns and are afraid of the unknown. They may not know how or what to change. If you are sick and tired of being sick and tired, then it is important to recognize the chains and begin questioning them.

I don't counsel people to lose weight when they are sick and tired of being sick and tired. Often the body has experienced so much trauma that it shuts down in a holding pattern. Your body is in survival mode and doesn't respond as you wish it would. This is a time to be very gentle and loving to yourself. Don't put extra pressure on yourself to lose weight.

This is about loving you the way you are—the weight you are, the height you are, the race you are, the *you* that you are. I'm really saying don't be too hard on yourself. Be compassionate with yourself. Changing behavior takes time. Sometimes it takes trial and error, and sometimes you have to get out of your comfort zone to find out what works for you.

Fourth, be in nature. There is something compelling about nature that speaks to every human being. It is important to put nature back into your life. You can do this by taking a walk or growing a garden—even if it is only a window box of herbs. If you are lucky, you may live by the water, a park, or an open field, where birds come and go with the seasons.

Nature can slow down the spinning in your mind. Being in nature has a way of calming the body and mind while accessing our interdependence and connectedness. Find out for yourself what your soul and body are telling you. Take the time to notice in nature. It just feels good. The more you let your soul drive the car of your life, the more practice you are getting in this new paradigm.

Being in nature can look different for different people. You might say, "I don't go out in nature; it is dirty. It's not how I grew up." Just notice the thoughts that are running your life. If you're outraged that dogs and cats are being mistreated, or that lions, dolphins, or whales are being slaughtered for sport, just notice that they are nature. Putting nature back in your life could look like protecting animals or the environment. Be open to your nature.

Being in nature can prevent eye strain, especially if you look at a computer screen, watch TV, or play video games. It improves sleep. The air outside is probably fresher than the air inside. It helps you stay grounded.

Fifth, I recommend meditation and relaxation. When you're spinning, it is very difficult to stop unless you are sick and tired of being sick and tired. Usually it takes a big wake-up call or an unexpected event to realize that you are spinning. Try meditation. You can get lots of meditation help on your computer. Or you might like to join a group of people who meet regularly to meditate. Joining a meditation group is a fun way to meet new people.

Meditation has been shown to help reduce stress and lower blood pressure. There are also moving meditations like tai chi.

Meditation is just one of many ways to relax other than watching TV. You can play a sport or take up a hobby. Popular hobbies include painting, knitting, crocheting, scrapbooking, model building, chess, skiing, sailing, or my favourite—cooking new and healthy recipes. I encourage everyone to use cooking as entertainment and relaxation. It is very relaxing to be creative.

Last, build healthy connections. If you are sick and tired of being sick and tired and you are learning about yourself, you may find out that many of your relationships are not healthy. It has been my experience that when you are on a journey of self-discovery, you need to surround yourself with healthy people. You may find that when you start asserting yourself, some of your friends stop calling because they can't push you around anymore. Shift does happen. It can be exciting. You may also find yourself outside of your comfort zone. This is a normal part of maturing in your journey. Letting go doesn't mean you don't care. It means you can't do it for someone else. Can you do it for you? That is the deeper conversation.

All of these suggestions are intended to help you build healthy connections, particularly your mind-body-soul connections. When all three are being honored and supported, things begin to shift.

Listen to your body. When you are in balance, feel for the goose bumps and chills. These are really good signs. Discern how they feel. When you are anxious, agitated, and uncomfortable, feel for the pit in your stomach, the tightness in your chest, the confusion. These are good signs too. Your body is trying to tell you something is wrong and you need to make changes. We often ignore these signs. It's time to bring all aspects of yourself into reverence and acknowledgment.

I can't stress enough how important it is to live a healthy lifestyle. When something happens in your life that is causing you great upset, it is hard to put your health first. You may not be eating, or what you are eating may not be nutritious. You may not be sleeping. You may not be getting out of bed. Just notice. What I know about the universe is that it is very patient. There will be lots of opportunities to practice and heal if you are willing to notice.

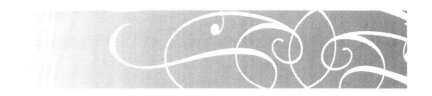

CHAPTER 14

Nightmares

When clients have nightmares, I recommend that they ask their nightmares what the nightmares are trying to tell them. Nightmares are normal. They have to do with anxiety, fear, and stress. It has been my experience that nightmares help people work out stressful or traumatic situations. Whenever I have had nightmares, it was because I wasn't moving forward and making the changes I needed to make in my life.

It is possible not to know something is bothering you. This is called *denial*. Human beings are very good at denial. Sometimes our denial is so strong that it takes a nightmare to wake us up to the need to deal with a situation.

For example, I had a client who was working and not enjoying their job. When they made changes in their employment, the nightmares went away. I encourage clients to listen to the nightmares and find the meaning. Often clients are not listening to their inner guidance and are doing things that are not loving to themselves or others. The person in my example didn't like their job, however they didn't want to leave their good income. Sometimes your health is worth more than money. They were able to find another job.

Ask your nightmares what they are trying to tell you and they will answer. It's important to honor the wisdom of your nightmares. If you don't acknowledge them and get their message, then they get louder, more horrific, and more disturbing. When you ask your nightmare what it is trying to tell you, be open to the message. It is different for everyone and in every case profound.

Nightmares are there to help you. Are you listening? Write down what you think your nightmare might be telling you. My experience is that people resist asking their nightmare. It seems ridiculous, too simplistic. Yet this method has worked for everyone I have worked with. It can work for you too if you are brave enough to deal with the answer.

People often know what they need to do, but they don't want to do it. Look at what is stopping you from doing what you know would be more loving to you. Expect thoughts like, "I have to admit I was wrong. I will be humiliated. I want them to love me. I am afraid to make the change." Find out what thought is there. Write it down. Let it come out and play in full view rather than hide.

I often share the saying, "Take the high road because all other roads lead nowhere." Keep being the highest version of yourself-love. When you are sick and tired of being sick and tired, you are often willing to try other ways, even if they are uncomfortable and appear weird. Just notice how invested you are in being right or stuck or unhappy. Who would you be if you were happy, free, and excited? Perhaps you think you would have to give up your identity—that part that makes you unique. You are holding on to a thought that is not helpful or loving to you.

Nightmares mean that something is coming up that needs to heal. It is just a matter of figuring out what that is. So don't be afraid of talking about your nightmares. Unconsciously, you are acknowledging them. By your acknowledgment, they let you know what they mean.

Nightmares are very exciting in my world because they mean things are coming up to heal. I do not see them as bad—quite the opposite. Nightmares have been very helpful when explored and addressed. In therapy, when someone shares a nightmare, it is always positive. It gives them direction for their healing. In our humanness, we can find the answers together.

Human beings are designed to heal, whether it is physically, emotionally, or psychologically. When people have challenges that are not being addressed, the meaning sometimes comes out in what I call "sideways." Some people have nightmares. Some people have digestion problems. Some people have bowel problems. Some people isolate themselves and hide out. Some people consider taking their own lives.

I'm not a doctor. However, my experience is that people often have physical responses to emotional pain and suffering. It's important to ask the right questions. Suffering can take many forms, but the content is the same. This is about ending the suffering in your world. It just might look a little different.

When people I have worked with start changing, taking 100 percent responsibility, and working with the thoughts that were running their lives, everything starts to change. For myself, my sensitivity to dairy kept decreasing. I can eat dairy today and not be distressed.

When you are sick and tired of being sick and tired and begin to slow down the spinning, things generally start shifting. Usually, something happens that will make you question if you really are making progress. That is the accordion of life. When this happens, you know you are making progress. It's a really good sign.

You know you can't go back because there is no "back" to go to. You don't want the past over again. You trust life, and your journey deepens. You are able to surrender to the frailties of being human. You notice what is keeping you suffering. You begin to recognize when divide and conquer are revealing war in your life. You become devoted to loving yourself first, not rescuing others.

Being the love of your life empowers you to love others from a place of wholeness, not emptiness. By taking responsibility for your health through sleep, nutrition, exercise, meditation, relaxation, a reverence for nature, and connection with life, things really start turning around.

It sounds like a lot. With support, it is much simpler than it sounds. As I said in the early part of this book, I like to serve a banquet of ideas. I encourage you to try these ideas out for yourself. Some will appeal to you while others may not. Sometimes just one shift can make all the difference. See what works for you. Ask you.

You are designed to heal, physically, emotionally, and psychologically. You are here to rise above what is happening or has happened in your life, not be defined by it. Express your true self and essence. We heal through relationships that express our love, beauty, knowledge, and compassion. No one and no circumstance gets to define you. Love is the highest expression of ourselves. Who do you want to be, love or fear?

CHAPTER 15

What Love Is and What Love Isn't

Pe=eople are often confused about what love really is. Many things can masquerade as love, which only adds to the confusion. Did you catch the ego trap *confusion*?

Generally speaking, love is responsibility, work, pleasure, commitment, caring, honesty, trust, communication, sharing, compromising, closeness, honoring differences, vulnerability, openness, respect, friendship, strong feelings, and more.

Generally speaking, love is *not* jealousy, possessiveness, pain, violence, obsession, selfishness, cruelty, dependency, giving up yourself, intimidation, fear, proving yourself, manipulation, or expecting all your needs to be met.

Can you hear the traps of the ego? I hear *unrealistic expectations, should, shouldn't,* and *excess.* What do you hear?

Sometimes we get confused, especially because most relationships start off happy and healthy and later become unhappy and unhealthy. By the time a relationship becomes unhealthy, the parties involved are very invested in the relationship. If there are children, there is even more at stake. People often think they should stay together for the children. However, it may be more important to show children what to do when relationships become unhealthy. You get to choose what to model for your children and the next generation. Perhaps love is teaching your children how to have healthy relationships and how to rebuild their lives if things become unhealthy.

Just like the many words we have to describe our feelings we have many different kinds of love. There is romantic sexual love, love a parent has for their child, love for a sibling or good friend, love of life that is playful, selfish love seeking fame and wealth and love of ourselves that helps us care for others and humanity.

When I stated that love is the answer to every question, I was referring to *unconditional love*, a love you give without expecting anything in return. It is also a love that you give to yourself that connects with and helps humanity. It is a love that knows the difference between meaning and power. What I am trying to capture is the difference between the meaning of life and the acquisition of power for its own sake. Perhaps more specifically, I'm talking about a divine love, your true identity.

What kind of love do you want to experience and give? What wars do you want to end? When you really don't want war anymore, things will shift in your life. A mature mind doesn't do war. When your response to life is love—and I don't mean being a doormat or a rescuer—you get to be whole, connected, confident, self-assured and able to be with all of life, even criticism. This is where your power lies. Love is the answer to every question.

CHAPTER 16

What Is a Healthy Relationship?

You may be thinking, "Why would she put this in here? It seems pretty obvious what a healthy relationship is." Well, you could be right. Generally it has been my experience that we don't think about what a healthy relationship is, or if the relationships we are in are healthy. People are distracted and tend to get caught up in the excitement and fun of a new relationship. They don't take the time to think through whether this relationship is good for them. In fact, your body releases hormones when you fall in love that make everything okay.

I had a client who had just started dating someone. My client went to the airport and missed their flight. They were so lost in the euphoria of love that they didn't hear their name being called, though they were sitting right beside the boarding entrance. All was well and it didn't matter in the least. Normally, they would have been very upset about such an occurrence. This time, everything was okay. (It helped that they were able to get on the very next flight!) Love can be a great drug.

Often people will say about a partner, "From the very first date, they laughed at me." Part of them knew it was not good. The other part wanted a partner in their lives. They were lonely or thought they couldn't be alone. It has been called "the warm body syndrome."

When unpleasant or painful things happened, they told themselves they were overreacting.

It happens more than you think. What have you told yourself to justify bad behavior from a partner, child, parent, or friend? Write it down.

Emotional abuse is the hardest to identify. There are no broken bones or bruises to show people. Others are often shocked and disbelieving when you share your concerns. Emotional abuse is covert, hidden, and even subversive. If you can't quite put your finger on it, yet feel like you can never do anything right, it is probably emotional abuse. There is also often a progression. Emotional abuse may start off as what I call "low grade" and escalate in frequency and severity over time. When an abusive partner is able to get away with emotional abuse, it just gets worse and worse. It is like the abuser needs to keep increasing the abuse to keep a necessary level of control or dominance on their side of the relationship.

My favorite example of emotional abuse is "going to the movies." It begins with the abusive partner saying something like, "Sweetheart, what movie do you want to see?"

The nonabusive partner says, "I would like to see this movie."

The abusive partner says, "I don't want to see that movie. How about this movie?"

The nonabusive partner responds, "Oh, that was one of my top three choices, just not my favorite. I wouldn't mind seeing that movie."

Weeks later, the abusive partner asks again, "Sweetheart, what movie do you want to see?"

The nonabusive partner says, "I really want to see this movie. It just came out, and it has gotten great reviews."

The abusive partner responds, "Oh. I thought I would take you to see this *other* movie."

The nonabusive partner says, "I just want to be with you. I don't care what movie we see."

Weeks later, the abusive partner asks their partner, "Sweetheart, what movie do you want to see?"

The nonabusive partner says, "Whatever movie you want to see."

The nonabusive partner has learned on some level that what they want doesn't matter. They may just want to keep the peace. And they may not be consciously aware that they've made the decision that it is easier to go along with their abusive partner than to express a preference.

Then the abusive partner asks, "Sweetheart, what movie do you want to see?"

And the nonabusive partner says, "Oh, I don't know."

As this continues, the nonabusive partner starts doubting themselves and really doesn't know what movies they want to see. They don't realize they have been undermined to a point where they don't have an opinion anymore—and if they did have an opinion, it wouldn't matter.

The next time, the abusive partner asks, "Sweetheart, what movie do you want to see?"

The nonabusive partner hesitates.

The abusive partner jumps in: "What's wrong with you? You used to know what movies you liked. You don't have an opinion? You're not the person I married. What's wrong with you?"

Have you noticed that the abusive partner has not raised their voice or used derogatory names? The nonabusive partner is left feeling not supported and not valued. They slowly lose who they are in the relationship. They feel it is not safe to say their opinion or be themselves. It is so insidious and progressive that the nonabusive partner just feels messed with. They can't really put their finger on what is wrong. It can take weeks, months, and even years to erode someone's self-esteem in this way.

Emotional abuse has many other forms. It can look like insults in front of others, jokes that appear funny, subtle put-downs, and "gaslighting"—leaving you thinking you are crazy or that everything is your fault. There are mind games and jealousy. In an emotionally abusive relationship, nothing ever gets resolved. The same problem comes up over and over again.

So what is a healthy relationship? It is a relationship built on equality. It includes negotiation built on mutual respect, conflict resolution, accepting change, and being able to compromise. Partners talk about situations and both opinions are valued and respected. You can have a difference of opinion, feelings, friends, and activities, and it can be okay. Money decisions are made together, ensuring both partners benefit from the financial arrangements. In healthy relationships, differences are celebrated and life goals of education, employment, and parenthood are supported.

Write down your thoughts and feelings as you read. Is your relationship healthy? What are you noticing? Write it down.

CHAPTER 17

Forgiveness

I have struggled with forgiveness for a very long time. I have read many books on forgiveness and how to forgive. When I was younger, I was told to forgive and forget, forgive but don't forget, forgive but don't let them do it again, and forgive for my sake.

I have grown to look at forgiveness differently. This means exploring the ideas that being human is not perfect; the role and liberation of our ego; consciousness; awareness of our true essence; seeing that we are not separate from each other; and acknowledging that love is the only answer to every question.

I have come to understand that the people who I think have "wronged me" or "hurt me" believe in their own suffering thoughts. It is not personal. They don't really see me. They can't see me because they can't see the true essence of themselves. The only thing they see are their own suffering thoughts projected onto me.

A deep feeling of compassion washes over me when I remind myself that they don't see me. In this healing journey, I often say, "Let the tears wash your heart." In this case, "Let the compassion wash over your heart." Feel it. Feel it now. If I believed what they believed, I would be acting just like they are acting. I would do what they do. When you understand that their fearful thoughts are running their lives, it brings compassion for them and yourself. Their fear comes in the form of inadequacy, unworthiness, insecurities, sadness, confusion, hurt, greed, anger, belief in scarcity, defense, attack, and war. Fear only brings them anxiety, panic, distrust, depression, heartache, emptiness, boredom, deep sorrow, misery and suffering.

I don't want to leave you with the impression that I don't think people should be accountable for breaking the law, violence, manipulation, deceit, taking advantage of others, or abusing their power. Being loving can mean holding someone accountable for their actions and following through with tough decisions.

I'm suggesting being open to walking in others' minds and having compassion for people who are hurting so much that they abandon their true nature. They have abandoned their essence of love. All behavior is purposeful. They believe that defensiveness, attack, and war will get them what they want. What a way to live your life. There must be a better way.

There is a better way. There is nothing to forgive. Understanding replaces forgiveness. You will feel about everything exactly the way you choose to feel, based on your decision about Who You Are, Why You Are Here, and how you wish to demonstrate your love.[10]

Love is the answer to every question. Pure love and the expression of love benefit the giver and the receiver. The giver of love experiences their true nature, their highest self, who they really are. There is no grander purpose of life. It is the ultimate expression of life.[11]

This is a win-win scenario. The receiver experiences the grace of how it feels to receive the expression of love. The giver is modeling and demonstrating the beauty, wonder, and joy of expressing love, their true nature.

Trust life. It will give you lots of opportunities to heal and practice. This is the best practice: to see the beauty, wonder, joy, and miracle in all things. It is true power and your birthright. Love is a choice. Love is the answer to every question.

CHAPTER 18

Shift Happens

This chapter reads differently than the prior chapters. A process of shifting occurs when you start to apply the concepts I have outlined. This shifting may cause a physically response. It can feel like an "a-ha" moment, a weight being lifted, or a sensation of lightness, floating, or airiness. I call this "the magic." Sometimes you have goose bumps and chills.

I don't always understand it. I just feel it and trust. When you have these sensations, it is important to realize you are not crazy. They are real. You may doubt them at first, however you will grow to respect them and live your life from that empowered place and feeling. This shifting occurs when a concept is identified and applied.

During a group session, when someone has a shift, all or most of the group members can feel the shift. Group is a safe place where people can be themselves, ask any question, feel respected, and be open to their shifts and the shifts of others. The energy in the room can shift. It is a good practice.

Here is a summary of key phrases that can be easily utilized to increase your awareness, insight, frequency of applying a concept, and experience of shifting at any moment in any situation.

1. ***One thought can keep you in an abusive relationship.*** This phrase is especially helpful when you are looking at what is stopping you from doing what you know is unsafe and unhealthy. One of my clients grew up with the fallout of their parents' divorce, and they did not want their children to experience divorce. They were able to see how this one thought kept them from making healthy choices and allowed them to stay in an abusive relationship. Once that thought was identified and questioned, they were able to leave the relationship and give their children a violence-free, chaos-free future.

This client was also repeating a family pattern. It has been my experience that families repeat patterns because the pattern is unconsciously what they know, and they are trying to heal their family of origin and themselves. They may think they are doing things differently, and indeed the pattern may have superficially different details. It is really important not to criticize yourself for repeating family patterns as they are coming up to heal. By identifying and questioning the thought you are open to other options and possibilities. Once you have felt the power that one thought has over you, you begin to notice other thoughts that are limiting, and that you have choices with regard to those thoughts too.

2. ***Let the tears wash your heart.*** This phrase has helped people release their tears. We often don't think tears have any function other than to show that we are weak. In our culture, crying is for sissies. It has been my experience that tears are one of the best signs that you are making progress. When you start to cry, you are letting yourself feel and acknowledge the hurt you have endured, the hurt you may have inflicted, or the pain you have been avoiding. It is the beginning of letting go—letting go of the sadness, the thoughts that control you, the hyper-vigilance, and the frantic, chaotic behaviors that you develop in order to cope. Sadness and pain are acceptable. Tears are therapeutic to the healing process. They honor the intense feelings that have been masked, releasing them and creating room to

let love come back into your heart. Sometimes we put shields around our hearts, hoping that will protect them. Unfortunately, shielding stops love from coming in and out of your heart, so you don't get to feel the love that is there.

Often people believe that once they start crying, they will never stop. You will stop when you have finished crying for all the things that you have not let yourself feel. Let the tears flow. Let them wash your heart of all the pain and suffering. Then your tears will stop. I have never known them to continue forever. You will feel lighter and peaceful when you are completely done crying. You have been holding them in for so long that they have become burdensome. Let it all go.

3. ***Whatever shows up, love that.*** Once you start letting go of your pain, you realize there is nothing you can't handle. Even when you think some experience is so terrible that you could never recover from it, you find the space to look at the good things that have come out of it.

There comes a sense of recognition of what you can change and what you can't change. You come to terms with each situation. If I don't like something and I can't change it, I look for why it's better than what I want. Choose life. If you have the courage to look, you will find it. I found it, many clients have found it, and you can find it too.

4. ***Love is the answer to every question.*** This is how I opened the book. I hope that it has stuck in your mind. I hope you can see that this is a deeper conversation. This is a conversation that is very human. This is a conversation that we have all come to explore and heal. It is the reason that makes sense to me why we are here: to heal the suffering by loving ourselves and one another. This love is not from a place of Pollyanna, rather from a place of practical, helpful wholeness. This is true empowerment based on action. It is

your gift to yourself and humanity. It is the ultimate expression of unconditional love. Love is the highest expression of ourselves.

5. *It's coming up to heal. Don't be afraid of your feelings.* When people come to therapy and start questioning, they often remember things that they had forgotten or that had been very traumatic. They often put events together that, in the past, were disconnected. When someone recalls a memory or has a nightmare, I remind people that it has come up to heal. It wouldn't come up if they were not ready to heal it. It is about trusting the healing process. When you start accepting and embracing what is in your life rather than wanting it to be different or running away from it, you may feel like you have just let a huge dam go. This is normal. It is more loving to you to trust and remind yourself that everything is coming up to heal because you are ready.

6. *You are never upset for the reason you think or say.*[12] This phrase helps you to question why you are upset. When I ask someone why they are upset, they usually give me a reason (a defense) for their upset. This reason or defense is uttered from the present; however, usually the upset is from the past. It is a pattern that we play out over and over again until it is healed. This is a deeper conversation. If you are willing to look, you can find the root of the upset. The current upset is a catalyst for going deeper into the past and your feelings. We replay the event in the hope that it will change. It will only change if we bring it to our awareness, recognize the pattern from the past, and choose a different future.

7. *When you give someone advice, know that the advice is actually for you.*[13] This is one of my personal favorite phrases to bring about a shift. It is a favorite for several reasons. First, when I bring this to people's attention, it shifts the focus from someone else to themselves, who is the actual person they can change. For example, I had a client who was very frustrated with their sibling. Their sibling lived with

their mother, and the sibling was mistreating their mother. The sibling was not keeping the home tidy, took their mother's money, and didn't have food in the house. Needless to say, my client was very upset. I asked them: Was their home not tidy? Were they not handling money well? Was there no food in their house? My client could see that their household was chaotic, they overspent habitually, and they couldn't keep food in their body. The details looked a little different, although they were able to see how everything they were upset about with their sibling was actually present in their own life.

This is a very powerful insight. Your upset is about something you can change. It shifts the focus from the other person to you.

Second, shifting the focus to yourself brings some compassion for the other person, because you are able to see how it is difficult to recognize what is going on unless you are willing to look and be conscious. Not everyone is sick and tired of being sick and tired—not yet. It helps you remember when you were not ready to shift.

Last, as a therapist, I find this is a good reminder to do my own work and look to see where I still need to work. Love is my practice.

8. ***As soon as you defend yourself, you are going to war.***[14] This is a very intense phrase. This phrase seems to be counterintuitive. If we disagree with someone, of course we have to give our side of the story. We feel obligated to try to convince them our way is better, even to the point of arguing. When you have the feeling that you want to defend yourself, notice that you start to feel uncomfortable, even if ever so slightly. Notice the pit in your stomach when someone flat-out disagrees with you and you try to convince them of your point of view. Be conscious enough to be with it and defend anyway.

Then be conscious enough to be with it and not defend yourself. See how that feels. Catch yourself when you experience the need to defend yourself. Catch yourself when the situation escalates. It could be escalating because the other person is abusive and this is the dance you both are stuck in. This is great practice for maintaining your peace and shifting. You don't have to defend yourself. It's okay to just let them have their opinion, especially when defending escalates and becomes habitual. Nothing is ever truly resolved with an abusive person. You just keep going around and around. You talk about it and discuss it and it never goes away.

For example, I had a client who was divorced. Their partner argued about everything: they couldn't settle the court documents; they wouldn't produce their income tax statements; they couldn't agree to a visitation schedule with the children; they wouldn't inform my client of accidents the children had in their care; they wouldn't help the children with their homework; they would pick up the children late, drop them off late, or cancel visits with no notice. Just about everything was an issue. Needless to say, this client was very frustrated. They stopped defending themselves, and everything shifted for them. They started asking for what they needed. They didn't give in or give up; rather, they stood in their truth. They approached every situation differently. They could only change themselves and their response. This is where their power lies.

9. ***You don't get to talk to me this way.*** This phrase is particularly helpful when dealing with an abusive person. Believe that you are worthy of being talked to respectfully, and if it doesn't happen, end the conversation. This may seem obvious, although it is not so obvious when you are stuck in the dance of trying to reason, compromise, and fix situations. You don't understand that it won't ever get resolved. You are dealing with an abusive and possibly narcissistic person. Then a light bulb goes on and an "a-ha" moment happens. It is important to stop the battle. Stop it in yourself and then stop it when dealing with others.

During a group therapy session, I had a client share that they used this statement with their daughter. They told their teenager, "You don't get to talk to me that way." Their daughter retorted, "I just did," and walked away. We all laughed. Nevertheless, their daughter got the point, and there was no argument. Their daughter knew what she was doing was inappropriate. She had to save face and walk away. Lovingly, there was a healthy boundary. You can say what is so for you without getting upset, defending, or having an argument.

10. ***Stop using other people to beat yourself up.*** This phrase addresses a deeper conversation. The deeper conversation is noticing if you are stuck in abusive relationships or stuck rescuing people, which may be a pattern of self-abuse. When you are able to stop defending yourself, when you don't let people talk in circles to you, you can see that you are the common factor. Taking 100 percent responsibility by looking at your role is setting healthy boundaries for yourself that will lead to change. If this describes you, then you may also notice how this permeates other relationships as well. If the relationship isn't with your ex-partner, maybe it is with a coworker. If it isn't with a coworker, perhaps it is with your parent. Write down the relationships that you find frustrating, difficult, or exhausting. You may notice that by spending so much time on them, you don't have to look at you. It's a great distraction and deflection.

11. ***Keep myself small and suffering.*** This phrase helps you to identify when you feel small or suffering. Your ego will use anything to keep you small and suffering. Write down where and when you are suffering. Look at your part in healing the suffering in your world. What did you notice? Is there a pattern? What does this remind you of or whom does it remind you of? Where did you learn this pattern?

12. ***Just notice.*** This phrase helps you to keep your focus. This journey is the journey within. Often we are stuck looking outside of ourselves for the solution. It is the journey within that is the way to

stop the spinning and being sick and tired of being sick and tired. Keep noticing what you complain about. If you don't think you complain, ask a friend what you complain about. It is easy to deny or not see who or what you complain about. Just notice and write it down.

13. ***You can choose to suffer or not.*** This phrase highlights that you have a choice, even when you don't think you do. When you are sick and tired of being sick and tired, you don't think you have a choice. You are spinning so fast that you can't see that there is another option. That is the ego's purpose for the spinning. For example, you can go to that family event and suffer—or not. You can go to work—or change your work. You can let someone else take away your peace—or not. You have a choice, even if you don't like either of the options. That's an example of double dipping. Did you catch it? Write down what makes you suffer. You can't change the situation, you can change what you make it mean. What do you make it mean? "They don't love me; they don't listen; they don't understand"? Write what is there for you.

14. ***Exercise discernment.*** This phrase reminds you to utilize and apply your new discernment. This takes practice. It often takes people twenty to thirty years to see there is a problem, exhaust their options, and then ask for help. When people ask for help, they are usually sick and tired of being sick and tired, and this does not feel good. The help I am recommending is not a quick fix. In fact, it takes some determination to look at things differently.

15. ***What you resist persists.*** This phrase reminds you that your situation is not going to go away unless you look at it. When you take the time to look at the situation differently rather than doing the same old same old, you will be surprised at the results.

16. ***You do until you don't.*** This phrase is a good reminder to show compassion to yourself and heighten your awareness. It is not meant as judgmental, defamatory, malicious, or vicious. Have you noticed your negative self-talk, the names you call yourself? Write down what you call yourself when you repeat a pattern or don't live up to your expectations. Look at those names and see if they are the same words you use to describe other people or situations. Are they words you would never say to anyone? If you notice you are very hard on yourself, then write it down and see if what you are telling yourself is helpful. This is an exercise of self-forgiveness and honoring that you are human. Human beings will make mistakes. This leads to the next phrase.

17. ***The universe will give you lots of practice.*** This phrase prompts you to realize that if you miss this opportunity to heal, there will be lots of other opportunities awaiting you in the future. I often joke that the universe calls down and asks, "Did you really get the lesson?" Let's see if you got it and can apply it to the next learning experience when faced with the same issue. Practice is important. We learn best through repetition; this is how we create patterns. When you are sick and tired of being sick and tired, it is time to create new, healthy patterns.

18. ***Be prepared to be wrong.*** When I use this phrase or am open to the idea that I may be wrong, I get a freedom that causes a shift. It's important to be okay with being wrong. The sky is not going to fall in if you are wrong. In fact, I have learned to enjoy being wrong. Being right can be very stifling. So you are right. Oh well! Sometimes being right feels very empty. If my experience has shown me what is likely to happen, I call it a predictable, probable outcome. I may say, "It is a predictable, probable outcome that your child will align with the abuser to survive." Your child will align with the abuser because they see the abuser as more powerful. People are surprised when it happens. I am wonderfully surprised when it doesn't happen.

In another example, a client was in an abusive relationship. I said, "The predictable, probable outcome is that the abuse will escalate if you return home. The abuser has already gotten away with it. They will do it again and perhaps be even more violent." When it happened, the client asked, "How did you know?" I responded, "It is a prediction based on my experience." Every once in a while, a client will come back and say their partner realized they have a problem and sought help, or their partner has moved out. I love it when this happens. I get to be wrong.

Another aspect of this phrase is noticing when being right covers everything that is wrong in your life. A client shared that they were fighting so hard to be okay or right, it created a kind of paralysis and a fear of being wrong. This conflict within themselves made them feel "crazy," inducing overwhelming anxiety. It became extremely difficult for them to make decisions or act where they could be wrong, especially when they knew in their gut what they thought was "right." Being allowed to be wrong was freeing. It allowed them to shift and liberate their awareness. This is actually another example of double dipping. No matter what they did, they were wrong. Did you catch it? Be with being wrong. Keep noticing.

19. ***Could they be right?*** This phrase is similar to the prior phrase. Sometimes wording it a little differently will give a better response. I call this "the juice." Find out what works better for you. When I am being criticized, I take a moment and really ask myself, "Could they be right?" It allows me to be present and see the value in the criticism. Sometimes, I just let them have their opinion. Other times there is some merit in what they are saying. If I go quickly to defend, I'm not open and learning.

This is a lesson I will continue to work with in my life. Being okay with criticism is a huge lesson. Criticism could stop me from writing this book. Grappling with criticism allows me to write. There will be people who don't find what I have shared helpful, and I'm okay with their opinion. They are entitled to their opinion even if it disagrees with mine. Just be with it. You are going to be okay if you are criticized.

20. ***You are living in a world that doesn't exist yet.*** This phrase is instrumental in staying present. It is very human to fear the future. We commonly bring the past into our future, and it robs us of the present. If you have experienced a traumatic event, it is very human to live your life from the trauma. Sometimes we don't even know that this is what is going on. You don't realize it until you heighten your awareness. For example, I was hit by a car. Afterward, every time I sat in the passenger side of the vehicle and a car came close to my side, I would put my hands on the dashboard and gasp. It took over a year for my response to shift. I had a client who was beaten and became hypervigilant to every arm raised or quick action. They were able to see how they were using this traumatic event in the past as a predictor of the future. They were able to not be defined by it and move past the event to create a much more loving future. What are you holding on to from the past that robs you of a loving future? Write it down.

21. ***Clean up your mess.*** This is fun phrase. We all make messes, whether in the kitchen, at home, or at work. I have different physical offices and I have a briefcase office. I usually sprawl the contents of my briefcase all over my office. I have a computer, power cords, files for group attendance, a file for intakes, files for administration, a hole punch, paper clips, and pens. It can look pretty messy. What mess do you have in your life? Often when people are sick and tired of being sick and tired, there a few messes to clean up. This could look like coming to group and doing things differently, apologizing to family members, dealing with loved ones differently, and making amends. This can also look like making better decisions, taking 100 percent responsibility for your part in the mess, stopping to notice, and focusing on what you can change: you.

22. ***Don't jump into their nightmare.*** This phrase is about keeping healthy boundaries. This is about keeping your wits about you. I often quote a little Hamlet: "Alas poor Yorick." I also quote a little of Rudyard Kipling's opening to the poem "If":

> If you can keep your head when all about you
> Are losing theirs …

It usually provides a little levity to the seriousness of the situation. This is another reminder to stay present and choose not to jump into fear. Sometimes people get stuck in old arguments and patterns of defensiveness, and the situation escalates to anger—particularly if they are sick and tired of being sick and tired. Sometimes you are jumping into someone else's business. They are entitled to their opinion. It doesn't mean they are right. There is no need to defend. Can you feel the pit in your stomach when you want to defend yourself? That is the old paradigm. Don't be seduced by the old patterns. You know how that feels: sick and tired of being sick and tired. You have had a taste of how freedom feels and being the love of your life. There will always be lots of opportunity to practice.

Or perhaps you are caught rescuing others? Do you remember what a rescue looks like?

- You are doing something for someone that they haven't asked you to do
- You are doing something for someone that they can do for themselves
- You are putting more energy into someone's problem than they are
- You realize that you don't really want to do what you're doing for them, and you come to resent them.

23. ***All behavior is purposeful.*** It is a reminder that even though a behavior doesn't make sense to me, it makes sense in some context. There is a payoff. It usually gets the person what they want. If they can't bully you anymore, perhaps they can withhold their love and approval. This reminder is especially helpful when dealing with someone who is unreasonable, contrary, irrational, or intolerant. This phrase provides a little space to shift your energy and your response to the situation. It can show you something about yourself and that there is a deeper level of conversation that is possible. There is often more going on than what we think. Instead of being angry or defensive—which is the beginning of suffering—it's important to see the action for what it is, not as something personal. Take a moment to pause. Perhaps it is a pattern of emotional abuse that requires you to look past your upset. It is important to apply it to yourself and your behavior as well as to the other person.

24. ***The form is different but the content is the same.*** Once you are able to grasp this concept and utilize it, you will start seeing deeper patterns in your life. It is a reminder that everything is interconnected and repetitive if you are willing to look. You are not crazy and not making things up. This phrase gets you to look at the situation as larger than yourself. It helps you navigate what was an impasse and reveal an experience of knowing.

25. ***You're allowed to ask for what you need.*** This phrase is particularly helpful when you feel like you have been shut down. It provides clarity in a confusing situation. There is no need to argue, get upset, or have a temper tantrum. Stand in your truth. Say what is so for you. Don't give in or give up. Be calm and clear. Breathe. It's not about giving in and it's not about giving up. It's about asking for what you need.

26. ***We sell out on ourselves for the love, approval, and appreciation of others.***[15] This is a phrase that packs a lot into thirteen words. We

are born helpless as infants and learned very quickly how to get what we wanted. At first we cried; then we learned words. In some families and situations, it isn't safe to ask for what you need. There are also times when what you want is not healthy. As a small child, you may want to stay up past midnight; however, bedtime routines are important and necessary. So you learned other ways to get what you want: being good, taking care of a family member, studying hard. Some ways are not so beneficial: acting out, being violent, and running away. When you are able to identify when you are selling out on yourself to get love from others, you begin to unravel your motives. As an adult, you don't have to do that anymore. This is a great reminder.

27. ***It is never wrong to love someone.*** This phrase is particularly helpful when people still love their abuser and don't understand why. It can be very confusing to still love the person who abused you. Further, when someone you love hurts another person you love, it is the most incomprehensible thing. Clients have indicated that witnessing an abuse is often as bad or worse than experiencing abuse directly, because you feel helpless to do anything about it. This is particularly difficult for children. When one parent is abusive to the other parent, the child's world does not make sense.

This phrase is a gentle reminder to stay in your truth. It is never wrong to love someone. Your true birthright is love. It doesn't mean that an abuser gets to continue doing what they are doing to you. It doesn't mean it is your fault. It doesn't mean you have to see them ever again. You decide, and you can change your mind. You get to do what is best for you. It may look different at different times. You also get to do what is best for your children.

28. ***The better you do, the better your children will do.*** When parents come to therapy, they often come because their children are acting out, struggling at school, and not following normal house

rules. The parents have tried everything they know and are usually exhausted. I remind them that their children are the barometers of the family. Some parents feel it's very selfish to work on themselves, and they often don't get the help they need to resolve their own issues. Helping their children is a roundabout way to give themselves permission to be the role models they want to be and to heal their childhood issues.

Children are always watching and learning. I encourage parents to look at it in two ways. First, how were they raised as children? Second, how are they raising their children? What role model do they want to be for their children? Write down how you were raised. Did you feel neglected? Did your needs not matter? Were your parents workaholic, alcoholic, or drug addicts? If they were, you were probably neglected and emotionally abused. Emotional abuse is one of the most difficult things for people to identify. When I ask people if they were abused as children, they usually say no. When I explore their concerns, there is generally some kind of abuse.

The gift of children is that they will show you everything you need to heal. They often know you better than you know yourself. Sometimes there is no other way for your children to reach you except by acting out. When your children see that you are doing better is usually when they do better too.

29. ***Your feelings are your way out of suffering.*** This phrase is a quick reminder that our feelings are the way out of being sick and tired of being sick and tired. Our addictions stem from suppressing our feelings. Letting your feelings out and dealing with them is the only way I know to move past sick and tired to create a new future. All of your feelings need to be expressed, even the ones you are not particularly proud of. It is very human and important to honor the whole emotional experience of being human. We often become very hard and unable to feel our feelings. We think we are protecting

ourselves. Actually, we are only feeding our addictions and feelings of inadequacy.

Generally speaking, you are either happy or sad or suffering or not suffering. It is about feeling your feelings, honoring them, and walking through them to healing. Walk through your feelings of being unhappy, fearful, or suffering. Get support. You are not alone. Walk through sad. Do it sad and get support. There is nothing you can't walk through with support. You have to acknowledge your feelings and feel your feelings. You don't have to do it alone.

If you slow down the spinning enough, you will notice that thinking comes before feeling. If you can catch your thinking before your feelings, you will have started a very empowering practice. You will learn that your thinking triggers your feelings. It's not the person or event, rather your thoughts about that person or event that are triggering your feelings. Keep noticing.

30. *I'm not my story.* This phrase encapsulates freedom from your past, freedom from fear, freedom from trauma, and freedom to live into a future that you didn't know was possible. The magic just keeps going. When one person moves past their story, it creates room for others.[16] It can change the world—your world. When I ask people what their life would look like without their story or what they want their life to look like, they are often at a loss. Their identity is so wrapped up in their story that they can't live or see past it. Telling your story and being your story are two different things. Are you sick and tired of your story? Does it get to define you? Who are you really?

31. *There is no "out there"; there is only "in here."* This phrase encourages you to focus on yourself. You change your world from within. You change your mind and you change your world. There is no other world than the world in your mind. Your life is a projection of what you think. If you think the world is a scary place, you will

keep creating a scary place and you will see where the world is scary. If you think there is hope, growth, and change, then you will see there is hope, growth, and change. Our minds are very powerful. What world do you want to see and create?

32. ***You are the only one you can change.*** Now you can shift your focus from blaming, reporting, discussing, condemning, and accusing others to something you can change—you! It is important to note that I am not recommending you be inactive in your life. I am suggesting being active! Volunteer, become a board member for a nonprofit organization, get an education, get another job, or run for political office. Follow your dreams. This is a deeper conversation of believing in yourself and your abilities. Love is action. It's not about giving in or giving up. Rather, it is about standing in your truth and acting from a place of clarity and strength. If you wait for someone else to change, you may be waiting for a very long time. You don't have to wait. Be the person you want them to be.

33. ***Hurt people hurt people.*** This phrase gets you to shift from trying to figure things out to accepting what you can't change. Who do you want to be? Write it down. Do you still want to hurt you or allow others to hurt you? Just keep noticing and write what comes up for you. Again, I'm not saying it is right. I'm saying it's important to move past their hurt and your hurt. Bring it back to what you can change and that is you.

34. ***Bad neighborhood. Take a right.*** This shift infuses a little bit of humor into your thinking. It helps you to recognize that your thinking is in a "bad neighborhood." You can take a right at the corner and choose a better, more loving and peaceful neighborhood. You are the driver of your life.

35. ***It's like drinking poison and expecting them to die.*** This is an old expression. It acknowledges that you are stuck obsessing about

them, yet somehow you are the one dying here. What you are doing is not working for you. Try something else unless you still want the same old same old.

36. ***Choose life not death.*** Very simply, choosing life is choosing peace, love, and forgiveness. Choosing death is choosing suffering, pain, lies, confusion, and fear. When you are confused, the simple way is often the quickest way out of confusion. Did you catch the ego trap of confusion? Keep noticing. This phrase helps you to identify what you want and to shift to it. Do you want life or death? The answer appears clear and simple. Often we choose death without being conscious of our choice. The choice is triggered by an event or the past. It is important to understand your thoughts—especially the unforgiving, fearful, and suffering thoughts—so that you can choose something different. It is important to look at what you were thinking about before you got anxious, sad, depressed, fearful, and angry. Write down what this brings up for you. To be human is to sometimes be ambivalent about wanting to live or die. Almost everyone has been overwhelmed by life at some point and thinks about death, including suicide. It doesn't mean you are crazy.

37. ***Life is all about death.*** This phrase refers to all the change in our lives. I first really started grappling with this concept when I was pregnant with my first child. I grieved my distended belly where life was being created. I grieved when the life inside of me was now outside of me and separate. Every stage that my child developed through was like a small death. I would just get a stage figured out and they would be off to the next stage. People would ask me which stage I liked best: infancy, toddler, latency, adolescence, or adult. I loved it all. They all had their gifts. Moving from stage to stage meant changing. It was exciting, unknown, and sometimes scary. Change is a type of death. I have a plaque in my office that says, "Don't be afraid of change, be afraid of not changing." Don't stay stuck. Where

are you stuck? Where is it that you don't want to change? Where did you die emotionally? When did you die emotionally? Write it down.

38. ***I would do those things too if I believed what they believed.*** There are two concepts being exposed in this phrase. First, it helps you to recognize that people don't always think like you think. Second, what they think is not always loving to themselves or you. If someone is abusing you, it is important to remember that they don't think like you. Not even close. If they did think like you, there would not be a problem. It is important to know what you think and then shift. You can only change you. If you thought the only way to make money was to cheat, then perhaps you would cheat. If you thought, "I'm going to get them before they get me," then perhaps you would get them first. If you think only negative thoughts, then you won't think other people think positive thoughts. If you think people don't like you, then you will find all the evidence that you need to support your hypothesis. "They didn't say hi to me when I entered the room. They didn't offer me anything to drink. They walked right past me."

These statements may all be true. However, you give them their meaning. To the person you are observing, the facts may mean something very different. Perhaps they just got a disturbing call before you arrived, and they were not present enough to acknowledge you entering the room. There may be many legitimate, loving reasons why someone didn't say hi to you when you entered the room that have nothing to do with whether they like you or not. A deeper conversation is that this is a different form of trying to understand. That is a trap of the ego. Did you catch it? Keep practicing when you are stuck trying to understand something that doesn't make sense to you. Realizing that it is a trap of the ego can help you shift.

39. ***If you are suffering, you are choosing pain over peace.*** This is what a lie feels like: suffering. If you think something shouldn't have happened and it did, then you are struggling with a trap of

the ego. Did you catch it? If you think someone shouldn't have died and they did, you are arguing with reality. Keep noticing when you choose pain, whether physical, emotional, or psychological. I'm not saying don't grieve. I'm saying notice if you're stuck. This can seem very simplistic and harsh, however it helps to recognize how you are feeling and what you can do about it. Write down your feelings, judgments, concerns, and distrust.

40. ***Everything you want from others, you can give to yourself.*** If you want approval from someone, you can give yourself the approval you want from them. You know you are a good person. You know that you are worthy. You know you have done your best. You know that you are only human, and your best today may not be the best you did a few years ago. This is acceptance and approval of yourself. You give it to you. Everything you want from them, you give it to you. You are the love of your life. You are the one you have been waiting for all your life.

41. ***It only takes one to heal, and that one is you.*** I have noticed that if I wait for someone else to heal, I will be waiting for a very long time. They may or may not heal. It is more loving and healthy for me to heal and not wait for someone else to heal or change.

42. ***It's a deeper conversation.*** This statement reminds me that if I take the time to look and slow down the spinning, there is always a deeper conversation. Things are often not as they appear. Circumstances may change. You don't have to keep reliving the past over and over again in a different form. An event in the past doesn't get to define you and take away your future. All of these are examples of a deeper conversation.

Another example I like to use is giving cookies. When I give you cookies that I have made, you don't know if I am giving them to you unconditionally, just because I want to share, or if I want you to like me. Only I know the difference. This is a deeper conversation. The act of giving cookies is the same, the meaning behind it is the deeper conversation. If you don't look, you will never find the deeper conversation.

What is your deeper conversation? When have you done something for someone just so they will like you? When have you done something you really didn't want to do, afraid that others would get angry or not like you if you didn't do that thing? Did you notice the rescue in the previous sentence?

What are you hiding? What are you afraid of? What don't you want people to know? What are you ashamed of? Only you know the answers to these questions. Be honest and look for the deeper conversation. You are the only one who can do this work for you.

43. ***You are loved much more than you know.*** Shift happens when you really understand that love is the answer to every question, and that you are loved much more than you know. There are opportunities all along the way to heighten your awareness if you are looking. Start looking for how you are loved. I often walk people though a guided meditation where they can feel supported. It starts with the chair they are sitting in. We are supported and loved by people we don't even know. If you are willing to look, you will find how you are loved.

I don't know you. Yet you are reading this book. My heart's desire is that you find this book helpful. People have edited this book and made suggestions so that you can make a different future for yourself. If that isn't love, what is it? Your ego will tell you that it's the job of authors and editors to write books; they don't really care about you. You ask you. What do you think in your heart? Who are you going to listen to, your ego or the love of your life?

What are you grateful for? Write it down. Who loves you? How are you being loved, whether right now or in the past, and by whom? Is it easier to accept pain or love? Write it down. Are you unlovable or tragically defective? Write it down.

44. ***Your peace is a thought away.*** This statement gets you to recognize that your peace can be a thought away. Your peace is close and available to you; you just haven't looked at it like that before. This is a new paradigm that has always been here; you just haven't accessed it yet. It is like my example of the bacteria and the microscope. Bacteria have always been here. We simply couldn't see them until the microscope was developed. Your happiness, your peace, and your freedom are in your mind, a thought away.

45. ***Your power lies in your choices.*** This is a continuation of the above statement. This is what 100 percent responsibility looks like. You are responsible for your choices. This is good because you can't blame anyone else. You may not like a choice you have made; however, you get to clean up your mess and make another choice. It is called making amends. It is very liberating, even if it is only liberating to yourself.

46. ***It's not good or bad.*** This phrase reminds you that most situations are not good or bad. They are what they are. We give everything its meaning. Practice seeing things with no judgment. Notice how it feels. Notice how your mind is squirming. You are very invested in describing a situation as being bad or wrong and you as being right and therefore good. Just notice how you feel. It takes practice.

47. ***Loving yourself:*** *what would that look like?* When I ask people what it would look like if they really loved themselves, they very seldom know. They often don't know how they want to be loved or what it means to truly love themselves. They are more invested in the idea that others don't love them. I start asking, "How do you

love others? Is that how you want to be loved?" They start grappling with their expectations of love and what it looks like for them to be loved and to give love. Often the response is, "Well, you know." And I say, "I don't know for you what love is, how it feels, or what it would look like." I encourage the whole group to meditate on it. If you really loved yourself what would it look like? What would you do differently? How would it look? How would it feel? Who would you be? Would your actions be in alignment with who you are? What actions would be loving to you? What do you need to do to be loving to you?

48. **You matter.** When I told a client that they mattered to me, they commented that no one had ever told them that before, and burst into tears. I told them, "Let the tears wash your heart." How would you feel if you really mattered to you? How would you feel if you really mattered to someone else? Do you only matter when you are performing, doing something for someone else? Is your worth wrapped up in what value you add to family, friends, work, and other relationships? Just notice what you do to matter. Just notice when you sell out on yourself for the approval of others.

Perhaps you matter just because you are here. Perhaps you don't have to do anything or be anything to be loved by yourself or others. Perhaps you were born enough and you matter because you were born. You don't have to do anything to earn someone's love. If you do have to do something to earn someone's love, then it's not true love. You are love. You have just forgotten. You have forgotten that you are an expression of love.

49. **Working it out.** I often intertwine my fingers when I say "working it out." This is a beautiful place of commitment to sharing ideas and suggestions to explore, coming together for resolution. In an abusive relationship, nothing ever truly gets resolved. The situation just stays in chaos, nebulous and unfathomable. Where are you committed to

working it out? What would it look like? What do you hope or need to work out? I often tell my children that there is nothing we can't work out together.

During group, I tell the members that I will disappoint them. I may say something they don't like. I might single someone out. I let them know that I am committed to working it out with them. They can tell me what is so for them, because I want group to be practice for them so they can take it out into their world. For some people, it is the first time someone has been willing to work it out. Most people's experience is that the other person wants to be right rather than work it out.

50. ***There is no time, only the present.*** Whenever I am rushing, running late, or anxious about being on time, I remind myself that there is no time. Somehow, I always make it and all is well. It is a gentle reminder that there is no place to be except right here. In this present moment, all is well. Just be with it and trust. During group therapy I use this phrase to remind everyone that the past is over, the future isn't here yet, and we only have the present moment. What kind of present moment do you want to have? Are you safe, peaceful, supported, nurtured, and encouraged to grow and strengthen? Just notice. What would it feel like? During group, I work very purposefully to create an environment where group members are supported, encouraged, and honored so they can feel it and create it for themselves outside of group.

51. ***What you are holding on to isn't worth holding on to.*** This is a gentle prompt to look at what you are holding on to. It actually may be hurting you emotionally, psychologically, or spiritually. Perhaps it is time to let go. Remember, letting go doesn't mean you don't care. It just means you can't do it for someone else. Can you do it for you? What do you need to let go of? Are you in someone else's business? Who are you still taking care of? Are you doing something they can

do for themselves? Are you doing something that they didn't ask you to do? Are you feeling resentful because you really don't want to do what someone has asked you to do?

52. ***Take the high road because all other roads lead nowhere.*** I have used this sentence because this is who I am. Whenever I am faced with a dilemma, I just remember to take the high road. All other roads lead nowhere. I don't feel good when I don't do my best or take the high road. I get to make mistakes, and I get to be human. I use this gentle reminder that I always have a choice, even if it doesn't look that way in the moment. Don't beat yourself up if your best on one day isn't as good as your best on another day. You will have lots of practice. Embrace your humanness and recommit to your highest self.

53. ***Fantasy Land is a great place to visit. I don't recommend you hang out there for long periods of time.*** This reminder brings a little lightness to your situation. We have all thought it would be nice if a person who hurt us were hit by a Mack truck or just disappeared somehow. That's Fantasy Land, and you get to be human. Just don't stay in Fantasy Land too long. It will eat you up and spit you out. Your ego will be running your life, not you. Shift as soon as you can. With practice, it will get easier. You will start to notice how you did things in the past and how you are making different choices now.

54. ***Not giving in, not giving up, rather standing in your truth.*** If you are stuck and don't know what to do, this is a great way to shift. Sometimes we think we have to give in, and we don't. Sometimes we just feel like giving up, and we don't. Stand in your truth. Say what is so for you; your heart. You may be wonderfully surprised.

55. ***What does that look like?*** What patterns are you noticing? What from your past does this present look like? You will start to notice that the past is recycled over and over again. What is possible is a

whole new future that isn't the past over again in a different form. When you say something, when you catch yourself, when you are complaining, when you are suffering—notice if it is a pattern that runs through your life. It probably is if you take the time to notice. What are you doing over and over again? What is appearing to happen to you over and over again? Does it look like the same old same old? Does it look like the past? Notice the patterns. If you look, you will notice the pattern, and by noticing the patterns, you can make a different choice.

56. ***Doing it differently.*** This is a gentle reminder that if you keep doing the same thing, you are going to get the same results. Doing something differently will feel uncomfortable because it is out of your comfort zone. However, it is the only way to heal your life. Doing it differently has many forms: asking for help from qualified people, following their suggestions, working on yourself first. You don't have to be defined by the past, your trauma, or anyone's opinion of you. You get to do it differently.

57. ***There is nothing to forgive.*** This can be a lot to take in. It is about replacing judgment with understanding and compassion. I'm not saying what happened was right. I'm not saying your abuser was justified in what they did. I'm saying if I thought like they think, I might do the same thing. Do you want to be right or do you want to be happy? I invite you to want to be happy. If you choose "being right," you may be choosing suffering. I don't want to be defined by what happened to me. I don't want to be defined by the past. I get to create a new future based on loving choices for myself. What are you choosing?

58. ***What have you noticed that makes you shift?*** Sometimes you will notice that a shift works for a while and then doesn't. This is normal. As you are growing, so are your shifts.

59. *Make a shift up for yourself*: _____

_____

60. ***Trust your journey.*** How did you get here? Did you ask to come to this earth? Some may say yes; others may say no. This is the confusion. It really only matters who you are going to be now. You get to choose. Choose life and your journey. It is the perfect journey for you to heal and be your true essence.

I often say that if you are in my world, you are in my world for a reason. I hope you have found the reason and some answers. I truly hope this book has been helpful to you. I have also written another book called *"What Are You Here to Heal? A Self-Reflective Guide"* that complements the concepts outlined in this book. It will help those who want to go even deeper into what they are here to heal. I wish you and everyone you love every happiness.

In summary, it is important to find out what works for you. These are shifts that I work with regularly with clients and in my own life to remain present and conscious. With practice, you will be surprised at how quickly these shifts work into discussion and action in your world. Remember, the universe is going to give you lots of situations and time to practice. If you miss an opportunity, it will present itself again, especially if you are looking for it.

Don't forget to have fun. This may seem like a lot of work or appear overwhelming. Just notice that that thought will keep you suffering. You can only really do one thing at a time. So just do one thing at a time. The same issue will come up over and over again in different forms until you heal it. This is really very good news. You've probably never looked at it like this before, you are here to heal all the suffering in your world. It starts with you and your world.

Love is the answer to every question. This is my love letter to you. Love has many forms. Love can seem confusing. Now you have discernment and some help. Did you catch the ego trap, *confusion*?

It's very exciting to see the many forms of love. Love can look like compassion for yourself and others. It can look like cookies. It can look like silence. It can look like a book. It can look like volunteer work. It can look like a hug. It can look like making amends. It can look like saying no. It can look like asking for what you need. It can look like the expression of your true self. The form is different but the content is the same. Almost anything can be loving.

I didn't think so on several occasions in my life. In each case, I was able to shift to see that the universe had something different and perhaps even better for me.

I choose life. I have learned to trust my journey, even when it's not what I think I want.

Wow. This is where my power lies: in my choices. You don't get to choose what happens. You get to choose what you make it mean. I would encourage you to choose love every time.

So there you have it, my banquet of ideas, suggestions, and experience served with compassion, support, and, of course, love. It is important to seek meaning, not power. Try them out and see what works for you.

There is no time. I am so comforted by this statement. There is no time. Feel that. You are in the perfect place where you are right now. The past is over, gone, nonexistent—not in a way that denies that it happened or mattered, rather in a way that refuses to let it define you. The only time there is, is now. You! You get to define you in this moment.

Who do you want to be in this moment? Do you want to be spinning, sick and tired of being sick and tired, racing from place to place or person to person? That is suffering. Suffering is in contradiction with who you really are. Do you want to be a body, only thinking of the material? Do you want to be the mind that creates and chooses your highest self, and trust the wonder that created you? You get to choose.

End the suffering in the world—your world. This is what you have come here to heal, to live your true identity and express the love that you are in this moment. I know you are being challenged by these concepts. Let your love wash over you. Breath. Relax. You have got this. Start with you and your world will change. Love is the highest expression of yourself and your true identity. You are love in human form. Love is the answer to every question.

ENDNOTES

Chapter 1: Sick and Tired of Being Sick and Tired

1   Byron Katie, "The School for The Work with Byron Katie," (Los Angeles: Byron Katie, Inc.), April 2008.

Chapter 2: Slow Down the Spinning

2   Byron Katie, "The School for The Work with Byron Katie," (Los Angeles: Byron Katie, Inc.), April 2008.

3   Helen Schucman and William Thetford, *A Course In Miracles Combined Volume*, third edition, (Mill Valley, CA: Foundation for Inner Peace, 2007), 110.

Chapter 9: The Form Is Different but the Content Is the Same

4   Neale Donald Walcsh, Neale Donald Walsh's Little Book of Life: A User's Manual, (Charlottesville, VA: Hampton Roads Publishing Company, Inc., 2010), 18.

5   Ibid.

Chapter 10: Old Paradigm: War – Divide and Conquer

6   Stephan Karpman, "Fairy Tales and Script Drama Analysis," Transactional Analysis Bulletin vol. 7, no. 26, (1968): 39-43.

Chapter 11: New Paradigm: Love – Inclusion and Acceptance

7   Jill D. Onedera & Bill Greenwalt, "Choice Theory: An Interview With Dr. William Glasser," The Family Journal vol. 15, (2007): 79-86.

8   Tony White, *Working with Suicidal Individuals: A Guide to Providing Understanding, Assessment and Support.* (Jessica Kingsley Publishers, 2011), 35-41.

9   Maslow, A.H. "A theory of human motivation," *Psychological Review*, vol. 50, (1943): 370-396.

Chapter 17: Forgiveness

10 Neal Donald Walcsh, Conversations with God, Book 4: Awaken the Species, (Rainbow Ridge Books, 2017), 230.

11 Ibid., 226.

Chapter 18: Shift Happens

12 Helen Schucman and William Thetford, *A Course In Miracles Combined Volume*, third edition, (Mill Valley, CA: Foundation for Inner Peace, 2007), 8.

13 Byron Katie, "The School for The Work with Byron Katie," (Los Angeles: Byron Katie, Inc.) April 2008.

14 Ibid.

15 Ibid.

16 Ibid.